Risk Assessment of Reinforcement Learning AI Systems

Looking Beyond the Technology

KYLE BUNCH, ALEXANDER C. HOU, RYAN HABERMAN,
MARISSA HERRON, ANTHONY JACQUES, GARY J. BRIGGS

Prepared for Office of the Under Secretary of Defense for Research and Engineering
Approved for public release; distribution is unlimited

RAND NATIONAL DEFENSE RESEARCH INSTITUTE

For more information on this publication, visit **www.rand.org/t/RRA1473-1**.

About RAND

The RAND Corporation is a research organization that develops solutions to public policy challenges to help make communities throughout the world safer and more secure, healthier and more prosperous. RAND is nonprofit, nonpartisan, and committed to the public interest. To learn more about RAND, visit www.rand.org.

Research Integrity

Our mission to help improve policy and decisionmaking through research and analysis is enabled through our core values of quality and objectivity and our unwavering commitment to the highest level of integrity and ethical behavior. To help ensure our research and analysis are rigorous, objective, and nonpartisan, we subject our research publications to a robust and exacting quality-assurance process; avoid both the appearance and reality of financial and other conflicts of interest through staff training, project screening, and a policy of mandatory disclosure; and pursue transparency in our research engagements through our commitment to the open publication of our research findings and recommendations, disclosure of the source of funding of published research, and policies to ensure intellectual independence. For more information, visit www.rand.org/about/principles.

RAND's publications do not necessarily reflect the opinions of its research clients and sponsors.

Published by the RAND Corporation, Santa Monica, Calif.

Library of Congress Cataloging-in-Publication Data is available for this publication.

ISBN: 978-1-9774-1315-4

Cover images: Asa Bingham/U.S. Army; Putilov_denis/Adobe Stock.

About This Report

This report discusses some of the challenges that the Department of Defense (DoD) may face in fielding an artificial intelligence technology called *reinforcement learning* (RL) in DoD applications. RL has been credited with expanding the decisionmaking ability of machines beyond that of humans in playing complex games of strategy. The fact that RL-enabled systems can beat world experts in these games raises the question of whether such systems could outperform humans in DoD applications. Especially relevant are "broad" applications that have large, complex processes with multiple steps leading to few but consequential decisions for a military commander. Timely alternatives could lead to decisive advantages in such situations. What is not clear, however, is what risks such a system would introduce from a technical standpoint (i.e., technical failure leading to mission failure) or the risks to the force structure incurred in absorbing such technology. This report represents a first step toward understanding such risks associated with employing RL-enabled systems for operational-level command and control.

The research reported here was completed in December 2022 and underwent security review with the sponsor and the Defense Office of Prepublication and Security Review before public release.

RAND National Security Research Division

This research was sponsored by the Office of the Under Secretary of Defense for Research and Engineering and conducted within the Acquisition and Technology Policy Center of the RAND National Security Research Division (NSRD), which operates the National Defense Research Institute (NDRI), a federally funded research and development center sponsored by the Office of the Secretary of Defense, the Joint Staff, the Unified Combatant Commands, the Navy, the Marine Corps, the defense agencies, and the defense intelligence enterprise.

For more information on the RAND Acquisition and Technology Policy Center, see www.rand.org/nsrd/atp or contact the director (contact information is provided on the webpage).

Acknowledgments

We would like to thank Jill Crisman in her sponsorship of this research; Joel Predd, Christopher Mouton, and Yun Kang for their continued assistance during this project; Wade Pulliam and Robert McFarland for their technical feedback; and the reviewers, Lance Menthe and Li Ang Zhang, for their time in giving helpful feedback that improved the report. Finally, special acknowledgments are given to the DoD fellows and RAND subject-matter experts who generously agreed to participate in the workshop held as part of this research; to

Clifford Grammich, who helped with the final workshop session; and to Peter Whitehead, Colin Smith, and Inez Khan, who participated in useful discussions.

Summary

In this report, we consider a subfield of artificial intelligence (AI) called *reinforcement learning* (RL) and the potential risks of incorporating this technology into the Department of Defense (DoD). Specifically, this report describes the risks to DoD missions as the size, complexity, and importance of the tasks performed by AI grow. AI has achieved remarkable success recently in a wide variety of applications, such as medicine, natural language processing, and autonomous driving. Some of the most notable examples are in the field of gaming, where AI has mastered such classic board games as chess and Go and complex online games, such as StarCraft II and Dota 2, in which multiple online players can play simultaneously. Common among these and other prominent examples is a learning component to AI, usually involving some form of RL. RL is a process by which agents interact with *models of the world*—in which the world is represented by a computer model—and are rewarded for behavior leading to desired outcomes. These successes have inspired great interest in applying RL to DoD applications as well.[1]

Throughout most of the report, the term *challenge* is used in connection with a task at which AI might be particularly prone to fail or cause problems during system operations. The choice of term is in recognition of the rapidly moving development in AI and the frequently failed prognostications that AI cannot solve certain problems or perform certain tasks. In this view, a *challenge* is an area in which an AI system is vulnerable and that DoD should analyze in greater detail because it may require additional technical development.

Risk, in this report, is a combination of factors: First, an AI failure occurs; second, the failure is not mitigated; and, third, the results of such unmitigated failure are consequential to the DoD mission in which the AI is used. Some risks are easy to identify, such as an autonomous driving system failing to recognize a damaged bridge, jeopardizing passenger safety, whereas others are more subtle and left to the daylong workshop, described in Chapter 4.

Unfortunately, many of the challenges and risks involved with fielding RL systems in DoD applications are unknown, especially those concerning force restructuring, RL system retraining, and mission impacts caused by potential technical failure. This report explores some of these issues using a notional RL application that provides decision analysis for a complex DoD mission. The scope and complexity of the application were chosen to encompass a variety of DoD disciplines to extract multiple challenges and consequences that might otherwise be overlooked through an initial assessment of technology feasibility. This application was analyzed through an all-day guided workshop using the participation of RAND Corporation technical experts and several DoD fellows who currently serve within the RAND community. Through this workshop, a range of important challenges were identified as likely candidates to consider in the use of RL within a complex DoD decision-based application.

[1] The term *AI* is used in this report in a generic sense, as it is commonly used. When we specifically discuss *RL*, this term is used instead.

Issues

- What are some of the primary technical challenges likely to be faced with developing and fielding RL in a complex DoD application?
- What are some of the primary nontechnical challenges, such as force restructuring caused by the fielding of RL, that DoD may face in using such a technology?
- What mitigation strategies, if any, could be used for such challenges, and what are the potential risks if they are not implemented?
- If mitigation includes retraining the RL to adapt to an unanticipated failure, how could the need for retraining be identified? Would this retraining be feasible when this failure occurred in the application?
- How do the identified challenges depend on the application scope (narrow or broad) and the rapidity of technology deployment?

Approach

We began with a literature review of RL to identify current technical challenges and successes faced by the RL community in developing applications using RL. This review consisted of both applications targeting mostly simulated environments (such as gaming) and commercial applications intended for eventual real-world operation (such as autonomous driving). Eight challenge areas were derived and summarized for use in a workshop consisting of primarily nontechnical DoD experts.

We then developed alternate scenarios to help explore the challenges and ramifications of deploying an RL-based system for a DoD application. To focus the exploration, we selected a complex, decision-based DoD application—operational-level command and control—that could present a diverse range of challenges to DoD force structure, deployment, and current state of technology. Such an application would present high consequences resulting from any expressed and unmitigated challenges identified. It would also allow DoD to consider RL technology in terms of application scope (i.e., "how big is too big?"), rough deployment time frames (i.e., "how fast is too fast?"), and issues potentially requiring long-term DoD investment or adaptation. Two scenarios were developed: one in which RL agents or systems are developed and deployed in a stepwise fashion over time, in a *crawl-walk-run* approach, and another that seeks to advance directly to the run stage in a *great leap* approach.

We then explored a guided workshop format designed to provide a useful forum for DoD participants to generate challenges and potential mitigations in the use of RL in the selected scenario. This framework would allow the free discussion of DoD participants who might have operational experience but little or no experience in AI. We considered first a formal risk-based framework to apply in our workshop, but our literature review found no such framework suited for AI and especially for determining risk within a high-consequence DoD setting.[2] Such a framework, if constructed, would be complicated by the poorly understood failure rates of RL and would have introduced unnecessary complication in our one-day workshop intended to generate a wide range of potential challenges. We decided to modify the framework developed in Mayer et al.[3] for our purposes.

The workshop was structured in three sessions over one day. The first session initially focused on challenges to the DoD force structure in the context of the crawl-walk-run and great leap scenarios. The technology was assumed to have gone through sufficient testing and validation to deem it suitable for deployment. Such an assumption was intended to move focus away from RL-specific technical challenges.

In the second session, the technical challenges derived through the literature review were provided for consideration rather than challenges generated from scratch. We considered this approach a more efficient use of time given that most participants were not familiar with RL. The challenges were used in the analysis as in the first session—i.e., consideration of the consequences and mitigations should the challenge present itself in the scenario provided. Finally, a session "hot wash" was used to discuss issues that the workshop participants felt were absent in the first two sessions. This session was further used to guide consideration of how some key challenges discussed were particularly aggravated by the broad nature of the scenario versus one that might accomplish the same mission in a more piecemeal fashion.

Key Findings

- DoD is likely limited in the use and development of RL because of the lack of specialized skill sets in this field and the difficulty in retaining personnel with such skills once obtained, given the highly competitive and lucrative nature of the field.
- The high data demands that scale with the size of the RL application may outstrip DoD's ability to train applications beyond ones that are narrower in scope.
- Issues coming from the black box decisional nature of RL and the reluctance of humans to trust the unintuitive nature of such systems may limit the size of applications to those that encompass processes currently performed by humans. Larger processes that humans cannot reasonably evaluate are likely to face issues with trust.
- RL has many additional challenges that expand as applications are broadened, including the growth of training sets and simulation models. Testing and evaluation (T&E) can become intractable in this case. Models of reality used to train RL cannot capture the complexity and variations of the physical world, and RL can fail unpredictably when it encounters situations deviating from its training. Thus, T&E can become a laborious

2 During final revisions of this report, the National Institute of Standards and Technology released a Risk Management Framework for AI, and we were unable to incorporate it. See National Institute of Standards and Technology, "Artificial Intelligence Risk Management Framework (AI RMF 1.0)," 2023.

3 Lauren A. Mayer, Jon Schmid, Sydney Litterer, and Marjory S. Blumenthal, *A Structured Elicitation Approach to Identify Technology-Based Challenges: With Application to Inform Force Planning for Technological Surprise*, RAND Corporation, RR-A701-1, 2021.

process of finding failure modes and subsequent training to force the RL system to perform as expected.

- Finally, while many solutions in the literature target individual challenge areas, the solution for all the challenges likely to exist in a broad DoD application was not found.

Recommendations

- DoD should explore ways to attract, train, and retain a workforce with the skill sets needed in RL. Given the cutting-edge and dynamic nature of RL technology, it is important to attract commensurate talent. Some of the skill sets gleaned from the literature include an ability to finely craft novel algorithms to solve specific problems; data engineering skills to train RL; modeling environments in which RL trains; and analytic skills to find failure examples in real-world testing environments with which to retrain RL or modify its algorithm. Attracting such talent may require changes to the force structure in a way to make DoD work in AI competitive with that in the private sector.
- DoD should develop ways to access and generate data relevant to DoD problems and required in training for RL algorithms. Such data must include operational data collected under the environments and situations in which RL is expected to function. Such datasets may be challenging to collect or generate if the RL system is expected to replace a process that, by its nature, does not have many examples from which to draw.
- Before being able to leverage the advantages of RL, DoD should better understand the limits of RL's application and how it provides an advantage over existing technology. Such understanding would include a process to adequately test and retrain RL in operational situations coupled with an ability to reduce expected risks to acceptable levels.
- DoD should consider leveraging incremental advances that are possible with narrow AI applied to smaller problems rather than initially pursuing potential advantages offered by broad AI applied to more-complex problems. Such an approach may incur less risk while offering a means to bootstrap training for broader AI.

Contents

About This Report ... iii
Summary ... v
Figures and Tables ... xi

CHAPTER 1
Narrow Versus Broad Artificial Intelligence and an Overview of Reinforcement Learning ... 1
Purpose ... 1
AI Versus ML Versus RL ... 2
Narrow Versus Broad AI ... 3
Machine Learning ... 4
Reinforcement Learning ... 5
A Taxonomy of RL ... 6
Gaming ... 7
The Use of Games as a Metaphor for DoD Strategic Applications ... 9
The Differences of Gaming from a Complex DoD Application and the Associated Risks of RL ... 12
Conclusions ... 17

CHAPTER 2
Further Technical Challenges of RL in Broader Problems ... 19
Failure in RL Systems ... 19
Lack of Domain Generalization ... 21
Domain Size and Computational Feasibility ... 21
Explainability and Trust ... 25
Reward Function ... 26
Vulnerability to Adversarial Attacks ... 28
Imitation Learning, Offline Training, Retraining ... 29
Autonomous Driving ... 30
Application Suitability of RL for Broad DoD Problems ... 37
Conclusions ... 41

CHAPTER 3
Scenarios for Exploring Challenges ... 43
The Application Domain ... 43
Crawl-Walk-Run Scenario ... 44
The Great Leap Scenario ... 46

CHAPTER 4
Challenge Identification Framework and Workshop 49
The Structured Elicitation Framework..... 49
Results 50
Additional Discussions..... 62

CHAPTER 5
Conclusions and Recommendations..... 63
Recommendations 64
Final Thoughts 68

APPENDIXES
A. Additional Workshop Details..... 69
B. Challenges, Implications, and Mitigation Strategies Identified in the Workshop..... 71

Abbreviations..... 77
References 79

Figures and Tables

Figures

1.1. The Classification of AI from Narrow to General 3
1.2. The Basic Concept of RL: A Rat Agent Learns to Navigate a Maze 5
1.3. Simplified Taxonomy of RL 6
1.4. Tactical Decision Domains 13
2.1. A Plot of Computing Power Needed over Time for AI 22
3.1. Air Tasking Cycle 44
3.2. Scenario Overview—Crawl-Walk-Run 45
3.3 Scenario Overview—the Great Leap 46
4.1. Force Restructuring—Average Impact on National Security Versus Average Likelihood 56
4.2. Force Restructuring—Average Impact on Operations Versus Average Likelihood 57
4.3. Two Employment Concepts Considered 59

Tables

1.1. Characteristics of Several Notable Games Solved by Computers 10
2.1. Risk Categories and Risk Factors in AI Failure 20
2.2. Power Estimations of Several Large DL Models 24
2.3. Examples of Commercial Applications Using Some Form of RL 31
2.4. Summary of Observed or Expected RL Risks for Three Types of Problems 39
4.1. The Categories and Descriptions for Rating Challenges 50
4.2. Top Three Challenges, by Priority, by Workshop Subsection 51
4.3. Top Force Restructuring Challenges 53
4.4. Graph Codes for Figures 4.1 and 4.2 58
4.5. Top Technical Challenges 60
A.1. Workshop Participant Backgrounds 70
A.2. Evaluation Statements and Definitions 70
B.1. Challenges Identified 71

CHAPTER 1

Narrow Versus Broad Artificial Intelligence and an Overview of Reinforcement Learning

Purpose

Artificial intelligence (AI) is a term often used to describe a machine that performs tasks normally reserved for human intelligence. Surprisingly, a formal definition of the term continues to be a topic of debate,[1] but this simplistic view is sufficient for this report, because it captures most, and perhaps too many, types of machine systems that perform tasks once limited to humans. AI definitions aside, this report regards what tasks may be problematic for current AI to do. *Problematic*, in this case, consists of twofold considerations: An AI system may be prone to failure in executing a task, and such failure may have consequences for the Department of Defense (DoD) such that DoD may be advised to develop AI to reduce such failure, develop strategies to mitigate the possibility of such failure, or consider alternative approaches.

This chapter discusses the concepts of narrow versus broad AI. *Narrow AI* is often used to describe AI built for specific, limited problems—an AI movie recommendation system, for example. *Broad AI* describes systems that solve more-complex and -general problems—an AI system that plays a variety of board games while engaging players in conversation would be an example of broad AI.[2] Narrow versus broad AI is important to DoD for at least two reasons: First, narrow AI tends to have a more limited scope of functionality than broad AI, allowing for more-thorough testing and a more limited range of mitigation strategies should failure occur. As AI broadens, it acquires greater functionality and more-numerous ways of failing. Testing to ensure acceptable performance can grow as well, along with the number of various mitigation strategies needed should failure exist. The second reason is that fail-

---

1 Dagmar Monett, Colin W. P. Lewis, and Kristinn R. Thórisson, eds., "Special Issue 'On Defining Artificial Intelligence'—Commentaries and Author's Response," *Journal of Artificial General Intelligence*, Vol. 11, No. 2, March 2, 2020.

2 In this report, *narrow* and *broad AI* are synonymous with being able to solve narrow and broad problems. While a broad AI system may be able to solve many narrow problems, the distinction is not useful in this report.

ure in the types of missions requiring broad AI is often more consequential and potentially more difficult to mitigate. An example is a narrow AI system maneuvering a drone to a target versus a broad AI system recommending courses of action in a wartime situation. Failure in the first may simply result in loss of the drone and be easily mitigated through redundancy. Failure in the second may be catastrophic and be irrecoverable.

An overview of machine learning (ML) and, more specifically, reinforcement learning (RL) follows; these areas of AI have experienced a tremendous surge in recent capabilities. One such area, that of gaming, is relevant for the success of RL to solve complex games of strategy and perform on the level of beating expert players. The validity and risks of using RL successes in gaming as an analogy for its use in DoD applications of strategy are discussed as applied to a battle management system. Various aspects of the analogy are discussed, along with the potential challenges and risks involved.

AI Versus ML Versus RL

Before proceeding, we need to define the following terms:

- *AI:* Artificial intelligence broadly captures different forms of machine intelligence. Marvin Minsky, one of the pioneers of AI, summarized the popular notion of AI as "machines that think."[3] Over the long history of AI, many different approaches have tried to accomplish this goal, and thus this term is broadly used to encompass them.[4]
- *ML:* Machine learning deals more specifically with machines that make inferences from data. Important is the concept of learning from data rather than being given a formula to make inferences.[5]
- *RL:* Reinforcement learning encompasses machines that learn through interaction with their environment.[6] RL is considered a subset of ML in that data are presented to the machine through this interactive process, with an additional component of feedback to guide the machine to improve its inferences.

---

[3] Susan Hassler, "Marvin Minsky and the Pursuit of Machine Understanding: Making Machines—and People—Think [Spectral Lines]," *IEEE Spectrum*, Vol. 53, No. 3, 2016, p. 7-7.

[4] Christoph Adami, "A Brief History of Artificial Intelligence Research," *Artificial Life*, Vol. 27, No. 2, 2021.

[5] See, for example, Anita C. Faul, *A Concise Introduction to Machine Learning*, CRC Press, 2019.

[6] Ahmad Hammoudeh, "A Concise Introduction to Reinforcement Learning," Princess Suamaya University for Technology, 2018.

Narrow Versus Broad AI

Many experts believe that the capabilities of AI will exceed those of humans in the relatively near future.[7] Indeed, recent progress of AI within the field of gaming involves complex, multiplayer games of strategy in which AI played at a level high enough to beat the best human players.[8] Many of the most notable examples of such advances involve some form RL, a subset of AI.[9] This progress leads naturally to extrapolating to future scenarios in which RL-based AI has broad intelligence, supplementing the decisionmaking processes of commanders within complex DoD scenarios.

As the terms *narrow* and *broad* are fuzzy in nature, it is useful to consider these terms further. Figure 1.1 illustrates a rough breakdown of capabilities that can contextualize the spectrum of AI from narrow capabilities to those that may eventually capture or exceed the capabilities of generalized intelligence.

FIGURE 1.1
The Classification of AI from Narrow to General

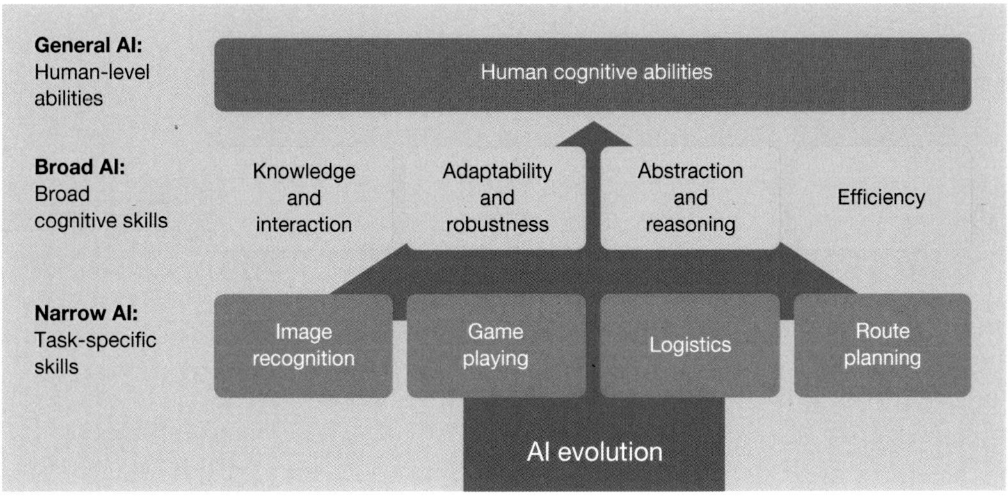

SOURCES: Adapted from Sepp Hochreiter, "Toward a Broad AI," *Communications of the ACM,* Association for Computing Machinery, Vol. 65, No. 4, 2022; and Yoshua Bengio, Yann Lecun, and Geoffrey Hinton, "Deep Learning for AI," *Communications of the ACM*, Association for Computing Machinery, Vol. 64, No. 7, 2021.

[7] Katja Grace, John Salvatier, Allan Dafoe, Baobao Zhang, and Owain Evans, "When Will AI Exceed Human Performance? Evidence from AI Experts," *Journal of Artificial Intelligence Research*, Vol. 62, 2018.

[8] Anil Ananthaswamy, "DeepMind AI Topples Experts at Complex Game Stratego," *Nature*, December 1, 2022.

[9] Qiyue Yin, Jun Yang, Wancheng Ni, Bin Liang, and Kaiqi Huang, "AI in Games: Techniques, Challenges and Opportunities," arXiv preprint arXiv:2111.07631, 2021.

AI ranges from narrow, task-specific skills, such as image recognition, to an algorithm consisting of a combination of broad cognitive skills. As Hochreiter writes, "A broad AI is a sophisticated and adaptive system, which successfully performs any cognitive task by virtue of its sensory perception, previous experience, and learned skills."[10] Such categories are not sharply defined, as demonstrated, for example, by ChatGPT,[11] a language model, normally considered narrow AI, that demonstrates some aspects of broad AI—i.e., holding conversations of knowledge and interaction.

In this report, we consider AI at two points in the capability spectrum, narrow and broad, and consider the challenges and potential risks involved in each. As the field is rapidly changing and diverse in its solutions, no one analysis can be considered definitive and fixed in its conclusions, especially without a more comprehensive analysis of specific DoD applications and capabilities.

This chapter describes narrow AI in terms of ML applications in gaming. Gaming is useful because it is well developed, can have highly complex features, and provides many challenges and insights into the performance of ML. Even with such features, however, gaming misses many properties present in the real world. One would not, for example, consider an algorithm trained in StarCraft as suited for managing an actual wartime situation. As StarCraft presents many aspects of the real world, however, one can ask, why not?

Machine Learning

ML is commonly divided into three general categories: supervised, unsupervised, semisupervised, and RL.[12] In supervised learning, the machine learns using labeled data by mapping inputs to outputs. This method lends itself to regression and classification problems.[13] Unsupervised learning does not involve labeled data. Instead, the machine learns with just the use of input data and seeks to identify patterns and associations, thereby making this method well suited for clustering and association problems.[14] Semisupervised learning is a mixture of unsupervised and supervised learning.[15]

---

[10] Hochreiter, 2022.

[11] OpenAI, "Introducing ChatGPT," *ChatGPT* blog, November 30, 2022.

[12] Radhey Shyam and Ria Singh, "A Taxonomy of Machine Learning Techniques," *Journal of Advancements in Robotics*, Vol. 8, December 28, 2021.

[13] Waseem Rawat and Zenghui Wang, "Deep Convolutional Neural Networks for Image Classification: A Comprehensive Review," *Neural Computation*, Vol. 29, No. 9, September 1, 2017.

[14] H. U. Dike, Y. Zhou, K. K. Deveerasetty, and Q. Wu, "Unsupervised Learning Based on Artificial Neural Network: A Review," *Proceedings of the 2018 IEEE International Conference on Cyborg and Bionic Systems (CBS)*, 2018.

[15] P. L. Bokonda, K. Ouazzani-Touhami, and N. Souissi, "Predictive Analysis Using Machine Learning: Review of Trends and Methods," paper presented at 2020 International Symposium on Advanced Electrical and Communication Technologies (ISAECT), 2020.

Reinforcement Learning

RL strives to learn as a living creature does, through interacting with its environment. It is analogous to B. F. Skinner's theory of *operant conditioning*, in which behavior is strengthened (weakened) through rewards (punishments) leading to the repetition (extinction) of behavior.[16] The classic explanation uses a rat as a model, and it is fitting to do the same to explain RL as shown in Figure 1.2. A rat (the agent) is placed in a maze environment to learn to navigate its way through. The environment governs the interaction of the rat in the maze. It defines the rules of how the rat can move (e.g., forward, backward, left, or right) and what rewards (cheese) and punishments (electric shocks) are applied wherever the rat may be (the state of the environment) in its journey. The goal of the rat is to gather as much cheese as it can while avoiding shocks by interacting with the environment and learning from the feedback. The rat does not necessarily know the best strategy (called a *policy*) to maximize its goal, but it continues to evaluate its state in the environment, take another action, and receive the resulting feedback. Though the rat's goal is not necessarily to complete the maze, it can do so through its interaction with the environment.

FIGURE 1.2
The Basic Concept of RL: A Rat Agent Learns to Navigate a Maze

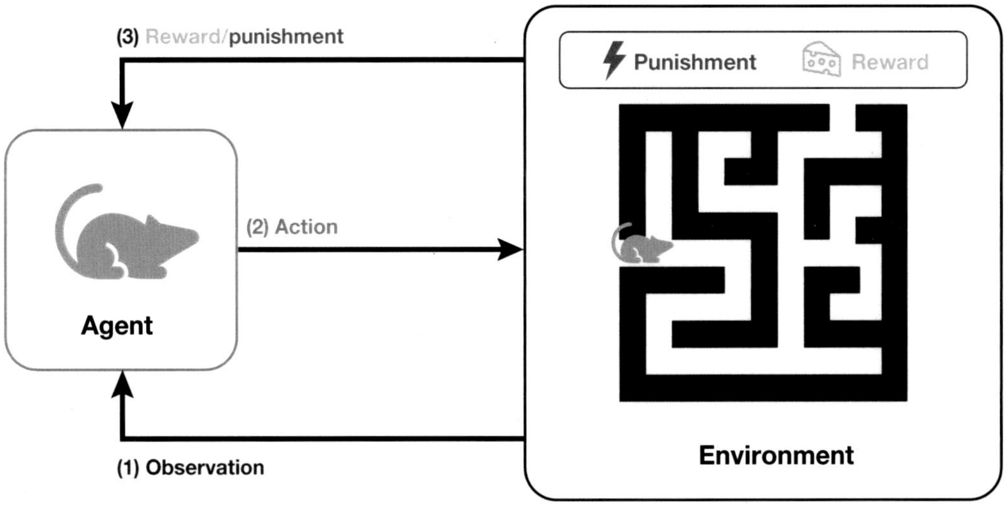

NOTE: The rat agent begins by making an observation of the environment (1). It takes an action (2), which results in a reward or punishment (3).

[16] Saul McLeod, "Skinner-Operant Conditioning," Simply Psychology, 2007.

In a similar vein to the above example, training a pet to perform an action can be considered RL. Providing the pet with a treat for the completion of a trick provides positive reinforcement that, over time, teaches the pet the trick. Similarly, negative reinforcement can be used to teach the pet to not perform an action, such as digging in the garden. The positive or negative reinforcement to a pet for the actions performed over time teaches the pet how to function within that environment.

A Taxonomy of RL

RL algorithms can be classified in multiple ways. A commonly used taxonomy begins with model-free and model-based RL algorithms (see Figure 1.3).[17] The model refers to whether knowledge exists regarding the dynamics of the interactions between the agent and the environment. Specifically, the model refers to the function that describes state changes and rewards. *Model-based* means that a model of the environment can be learned or has already been learned and is, thus, provided (e.g., chess).[18] Understanding the dynamics in an environment enables anticipation or prediction of an agent's future actions toward success. The

FIGURE 1.3
Simplified Taxonomy of RL

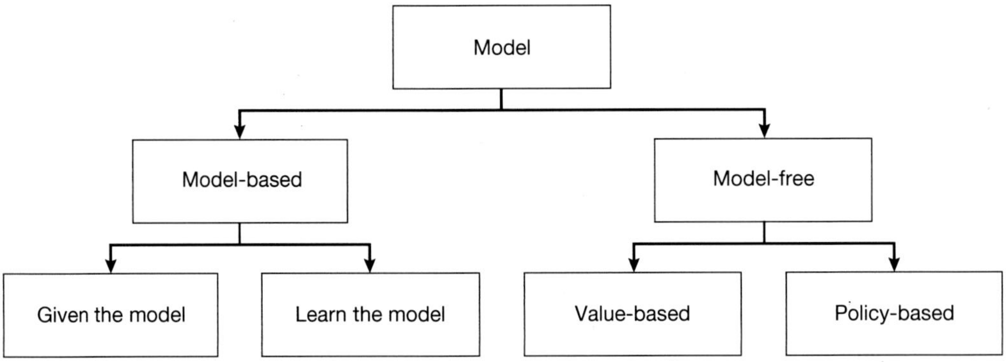

SOURCE: Adapted from Hao Dong, Zihan Ding, and Shanghang Zhang, *Deep Reinforcement Learning: Fundamentals, Research and Application*, Springer, 2020.

[17] Dong, Ding, and Zhang, 2020.

[18] Fan-Ming Luo, Tian Xu, Hang Lai, Xiong-Hui Chen, Weinan Zhang, and Yang Yu, "A Survey on Model-Based Reinforcement Learning," eprint arXiv:2206.0932, June 2022; C. V. Pal and F. Leon, "Brief Survey of Model-Based Reinforcement Learning Techniques," *Proceedings of the 24th International Conference on System Theory, Control and Computing (ICSTCC)*, 2020.

ability to predict then allows the agent to learn a policy. A well-understood model that provides an understanding of the agent-environment dynamics will require fewer example scenarios to create the policy.[19] Instead, the model-based algorithms focus on choosing a policy that best fits the modeled environment. Model-free algorithms are, as the name suggests, without a modeled environment. They often exist when the environment is too complex to model. These algorithms instead focus on selecting a policy as the agent experiences the environment. In other words, the agent pursues a trial-and-error approach in the environment, and the policy is selected according to the results of that approach.[20] Model-free algorithms can be value-based or policy-based. *Value-based* algorithms strive to learn the accumulated future reward for any move from a particular state. A *policy-based* algorithm strives to learn the policy directly.

Two key concepts in RL are exploration and exploitation. *Exploration* refers to the agent trying new interactions with the environment to learn more about the environment. The interactions may not produce the best immediate rewards but may identify new interactions and decisions that can lead to a greater long-term reward. *Exploitation*, in contrast, means that the agent interacts with the environment by selecting the action that produces the best immediate or short-term reward. The short-term focus of exploitation means the agent functions based only on its current knowledge of the environment and does not consider potential gains from future knowledge (through exploration) of the environment. A trade-off between the immediate benefits of exploitation and the uncertain potential gain from exploration is a reoccurring concept throughout RL and will be considered later.

Gaming

The use of AI to solve games carries with it several advantages. First, the rules of the game are known and can range from very simple (tic-tac-toe) to very complex (online virtual reality with multiple players, different strategies for winning, and so on). Second, the environments can also range from simple (checkers) to quite complex (virtual reality–type games), but this same environment is generated by a computer, allowing the generation of testing examples constrained by computational power and any limitations in either strategies for winning or examples for training. In games like tic-tac-toe, for example, a computer can generate all possible game combinations and determine plays for each that maximize the outcome of the game. It does not take a big leap in complexity for such an approach (i.e., determine all possible outcomes for all possible games) to outstrip computational ability. Chess is one such game, but it is still possible to use sophisticated tree search methods that project possible forward moves and to select the ones more likely to win against an opponent. Such was the

[19] Lex Fridman, "MIT 6.S091: Introduction to Deep Reinforcement Learning (Deep RL)," video, 2019.

[20] Louis Owen, "Bird's-Eye View of Reinforcement Learning Algorithms Taxonomy," *Towards Data Science*, October 30, 2020.

strategy that led to the famous win of IBM's Deep Blue algorithm against the grandmaster Garry Kasparov in 1997.[21] Deep Blue was designed as a computer that specialized in playing chess using sophisticated search methods coupled with a complex selection of forward move strategy.[22] Deep Blue was such a success that Kasparov expressed doubts that he was playing a machine.[23]

AlphaGo

While the victory of Deep Blue represented a major milestone in AI, the game of Go is considered considerably more challenging in the number of possible moves and strategies for winning. For example, chess has approximately 80 moves per game and Go 300. The *branching factor* or number of moves possible from particular points (beginning, middle, end) is ~35 in chess versus ~300 in Go. The end state in chess for scoring is simple (checkmate) and in Go more complex—counting territory, or consensus by players. The rules are simple, but the result is complex.[24]

In 2015, the algorithm called AlphaGo won against the reigning three-time European champion, Fan Hui.[25] This win represented a major turning point in AI and was followed by another win a year later against the Chinese Go champion Ke Jie, who stated,

> To me, AlphaGo is a god, a being that can defeat anyone or anything. What he sees is the whole universe, while what we see is just a pond in front of us.[26]

The AlphaGo algorithm is clearly explained in Silver et al.[27] AlphaGo was based on a combination of approaches coupled with RL. First, prior work on expert play was used in a supervised learning approach to train a neural network. Board states were selected randomly as input. The result predicted expert moves approximately 56 percent versus 44 percent of the

---

[21] Feng-Hsiung Hsu, "IBM's Deep Blue Chess Grandmaster Chips," *IEEE Micro*, Vol. 19, No. 2, 1999.

[22] Murray Campbell, "Knowledge Discovery in Deep Blue," *Communications of the ACM*, Association for Computing Machinery, Vol. 42, No. 11, 1999.

[23] G. Buttazzo, "Artificial Consciousness: Utopia or Real Possibility?" *Computer*, Vol. 34, No. 7, 2001.

[24] J. Burmeister and J. Wiles, "The Challenge of Go as a Domain for AI Research: A Comparison Between Go and Chess," *Proceedings of Third Australian and New Zealand Conference on Intelligent Information Systems*, 1995.

[25] Christof Koch, "How the Computer Beat the Go Player," *Scientific American Mind*, July 1, 2016.

[26] Quoted in Paolo Bory, "Deep New: The Shifting Narratives of Artificial Intelligence from Deep Blue to AlphaGo," *Convergence*, Vol. 25, No. 4, 2019.

[27] David Silver, Aja Huang, Chris J. Maddison, Arthur Guez, Laurent Sifre, George van den Driessche, Julian Schrittwieser, Ioannis Antonoglou, Veda Panneershelvam, Marc Lanctot, Sander Dieleman, Dominik Grewe, John Nham, Nal Kalchbrenner, Ilya Sutskever, Timothy Lillicrap, Madeleine Leach, Koray Kavukcuoglu, Thore Graepel, and Demis Hassabis, "Mastering the Game of Go with Deep Neural Networks and Tree Search," *Nature*, Vol. 529, No. 7587, January 1, 2016.

then–state of the art. Tuning of the neural network by increasing its size improved accuracy, but smaller networks were considerably faster, with an accuracy of just 24.2 percent. These were subsequently used in a complex training pipeline of random tree searching and computer game play to improve the RL network.

AlphaGo Zero

Whereas AlphaGo leveraged expert play to bootstrap the training of a neural network, a subsequent algorithm called AlphaGo Zero did not use a supervised learning approach and trained completely from self-play.[28] It used a random tree search to select moves coupled with the subsequent winner of the self-played games to improve its policy. Training was distributed over many machines, each having four specialized tensor processing units.[29] The algorithm trained continuously for three days over approximately 3.9 million games to beat the existing machine champion.

Dota 2

The demonstrations and progress of RL in gaming continue with, for example, RL algorithms beating online virtual game masters in the game Dota 2.[30] Here, the virtual game has multiple simultaneous players, a complex environment and rules, and many other characteristics associated with actual real-world situations. As before, training requirements are computationally high, this time with thousands of specialized processors over a ten-month training period.

The Use of Games as a Metaphor for DoD Strategic Applications

The previous section was a sample of significant advances in computer gaming, but it is certainly not comprehensive.[31] RL is a component of many of the recent advances in train-

---

[28] David Silver, Julian Schrittwieser, Karen Simonyan, Ioannis Antonoglou, Aja Huang, Arthur Guez, Thomas Hubert, Lucas Baker, Matthew Lai, Adrian Bolton, Yutian Chen, Timothy Lillicrap, Fan Hui, Laurent Sifre, George van den Driessche, Thore Graepel, and Demis Hassabis, "Mastering the Game of Go Without Human Knowledge," *Nature*, Vol. 550, No. 7676, October 1, 2017.

[29] Tensor processing units are computer chips specialized for ML algorithms. See Norman P. Jouppi, Cliff Young, Nishant Patil, David Patterson, Gaurav Agrawal, Raminder Bajwa, Sarah Bates, Suresh Bhatia, Nan Boden, and Al Borchers, "In-Datacenter Performance Analysis of a Tensor Processing Unit," *Proceedings of the 44th Annual International Symposium on Computer Architecture*, 2017.

[30] Christopher Berner, Greg Brockman, Brooke Chan, Vicki Cheung, Przemysław Dębiak, Christy Dennison, David Farhi, Quirin Fischer, Shariq Hashme, and Chris Hesse, "Dota 2 with Large Scale Deep Reinforcement Learning," arXiv preprint arXiv:1912.06680, 2019.

[31] Yin et al., 2021.

ing deep neural networks to win at games of strategy in various situations of complexity in the environment, rules, number and cooperative strategies of players and various forms of unknown information within the game, such as hidden cards in games of poker or incomplete views of the game, as in Dota 2. In many cases, such as in games of Go, the question is not so much whether computers can beat humans but rather which algorithm is able to beat the others. In such an environment it becomes natural to consider the utility of RL to DoD applications that involve strategic decisionmaking.

To better guide this discussion, it is useful to list the characteristics of some of the notable advances in gaming with respect to characteristics that presented a challenge to overcome, as shown in Table 1.1.

The order of the table is roughly by the challenge of the overall game as presented to an AI system. As listed, these challenges include the following:

- *the number of game players and whether there is cooperative play.* Generally, the complexity of games increases as the number of players increases. Further, the potential for cooperative teams in such games as Dota 2 forces decisions as to how advantage might be gained through team playing.
- *the measure of the state space of the game and the game's horizon. State space* is a rough measure of the size of the game using the number of legal positions possible in the game from its initial configuration. *Horizon* is a measure of the number of moves on average until completion. Chess, for example, begins with the same initial position for each game, but its game variations quickly grow with each move. As shown in Table 1.1, on average, it takes about 80 moves to complete a game. The number of state spaces grows rapidly as the number of board positions increases and the rules allow long play hori-

TABLE 1.1
Characteristics of Several Notable Games Solved by Computers

Game	Players	Board	State Space	Real Time	Information	Stochasticity	Player Cooperation	Horizon
Chess	2	8x8	1,047	No	Perfect	Deterministic	No	~80
Go	2	19x19	10,170	No	Perfect	Deterministic	No	~300
Poker	2 or more	Card	10,161	No	Imperfect	Stochastic	No	Varies[a]
StarCraft	2	Video	101,685	Yes	Imperfect	Stochastic	No	Long
Dota 2	10	Video	[b]	Yes	Imperfect	Stochastic	Yes	Long

SOURCES: Features data from Aske Plaat, *Learning to Play: Reinforcement Learning and Games*, Springer Nature, 2020; Yin et al., 2021; and Yunlong Lu and Wenxin Li, "Techniques and Paradigms in Modern Game AI Systems," *Algorithms*, Vol. 15, No. 8, 2022.

[a] The horizon of poker varies considerably by its variations and number of players (Michael Johanson, "Measuring the Size of Large No-Limit Poker Games," arXiv preprint arXiv:1302.7008, 2013).

[b] State space estimates not found.

zons (Go) or the game allows multiple initial conditions in players and rules (variations of poker).

- *the real-time nature of such games as StarCraft and Dota 2.* Real-time games of strategy present several challenges,[32] one of which is that indecision or delayed decision can cause game losses because one or more players can capitalize on such delays.
- *games of perfect or imperfect information.* Chess is a game of *perfect* information, in which the players see the entire board and the moves of the opponent. Information is not hidden in this case. In *imperfect* games, such as in poker, players have information that is not known to the others. Formulating a strategy in this case involves guessing what cards an opponent might have and leveraging the uncertainty of the opponent as to one's own set of cards. Games of imperfect information provide challenges in terms of the growth of potential moves (plays) possible when projecting forward in the game and the time needed to calculate an optimal strategy.[33]
- *games with stochastic elements.* Adding the roll of a die or the shuffling of cards to a game adds a random element to the game. According to Solan and Vieille,

> The complexity of stochastic games stems from the fact that the choices made by the players have two, sometimes contradictory, effects. First, together with the current state, the players' actions determine the immediate payoff that each player receives. Second, the current state and the players' actions influence the choice of the new state, which determines the potential of future payoffs. In particular, when choosing his actions, each player has to balance these forces, a decision that may often be difficult. Although this dichotomy is also present in one-player sequential decision problems, the presence of additional players who maximize their own goals adds complexity to the analysis of the situation.[34]

Stochastic games can vary in difficulty depending on the type of game and how the stochastic element is introduced.[35]

The use of RL in solving games has progressed along many dimensions of increasing complexity to where it is natural to consider these examples as indicative of RL's suitability for decision support in DoD scenarios. The next section describes how such an application can differ from a complex gaming scenario and the potential risks that may result.

---

[32] Santiago Ontañón, Gabriel Synnaeve, Alberto Uriarte, Florian Richoux, David Churchill, and Mike Preuss, "RTS AI Problems and Techniques," in Newton Lee, ed., *Encyclopedia of Computer Graphics and Games*, Springer International Publishing, 2015.

[33] Neil Burch, "Time and Space: Why Imperfect Information Games Are Hard," thesis, University of Alberta, 2018.

[34] Eilon Solan and Nicolas Vieille, "Stochastic Games," *Proceedings of the National Academy of Sciences*, Vol. 112, No. 45, 2015.

[35] Diogo M. Costa, "Computational Complexity of Games and Puzzles," master's thesis, Harvard University, July 2018; Marcin Przybylko, *Stochastic Games and Their Complexities*, Nouvelle Calédonie, 2019; Constantinos Daskalakis, Noah Golowich, and Kaiqing Zhang, "The Complexity of Markov Equilibrium in Stochastic Games," unpublished manuscript, April 2022.

The Differences of Gaming from a Complex DoD Application and the Associated Risks of RL

Johnson and Treadway considered the use of AI in a tactical battlefield management system.[36] Such a system would draw from a range of different domains to make tactical decisions on the battlefield, as shown in Figure 1.4.

On a cursory level, many of the elements of this system are present to a smaller degree in games such as StarCraft and Dota 2, which have been played using RL. Such games can have multiplayer strategies operating in complex spatial domains. Some have complex constraints and rules, and the game unfolds in real time over a significant period. Consider the following challenges and risks in applying the gaming metaphor to this application.

In Gaming, the Game Is Reality

Games are essentially complete within their own universe. While it is true that in a game such as chess, a physical instance of the game exists, no reason exists to assume that a computer representation of the game would lack some element of the game important to its play. Such is not the case for a computer simulation of the complex mix of domains shown in Figure 1.4. An RL system trained under battle learns from a representation of reality. As good as such a computer simulation may be, risks may be introduced in the following forms:

- Bias.[37] A simulated battle scenario might contain unintended biases from the architects of the scenario. For example, would the rules and policies that guide or govern the Blue team response also bias the simulated behavior of the Red team?[38]
- Missing or incomplete information. Many elements within the spatial domains of Figure 1.4 can be difficult or impossible to accurately simulate. Such complexities are abstracted to simpler equivalents, but they may lose information important to the learning process of the RL. For example, roads abstracted to be always passable might teach the RL incorrect lessons on the difficulty of logistics in actual conditions that may guide incorrect tactical decisions on ground force availability. Incomplete information on Red team capabilities may result in simulations that underestimate the Red team, leading to poor tactical decisions from the resulting RL.
- Too much or irrelevant information. Simulations must always balance what is relevant for RL training against what is irrelevant. Ideally, an RL algorithm would learn rapidly

---

[36] Bonnie Johnson and William A. Treadway, "Artificial Intelligence—an Enabler of Naval Tactical Decision Superiority," *AI Magazine*, Vol. 40, No. 1, 2019.

[37] G. Hailu and G. Sommer, "On Amount and Quality of Bias in Reinforcement Learning," *Proceedings of the IEEE SMC'99 Conference Proceedings: 1999 IEEE International Conference on Systems, Man, and Cybernetics* (Cat. No. 99CH37028), Vol. 722, 1999.

[38] *Blue* and *Red teams* are customary terms to signify two opposing forces, with generally the Blue team being the favored side.

FIGURE 1.4
Tactical Decision Domains

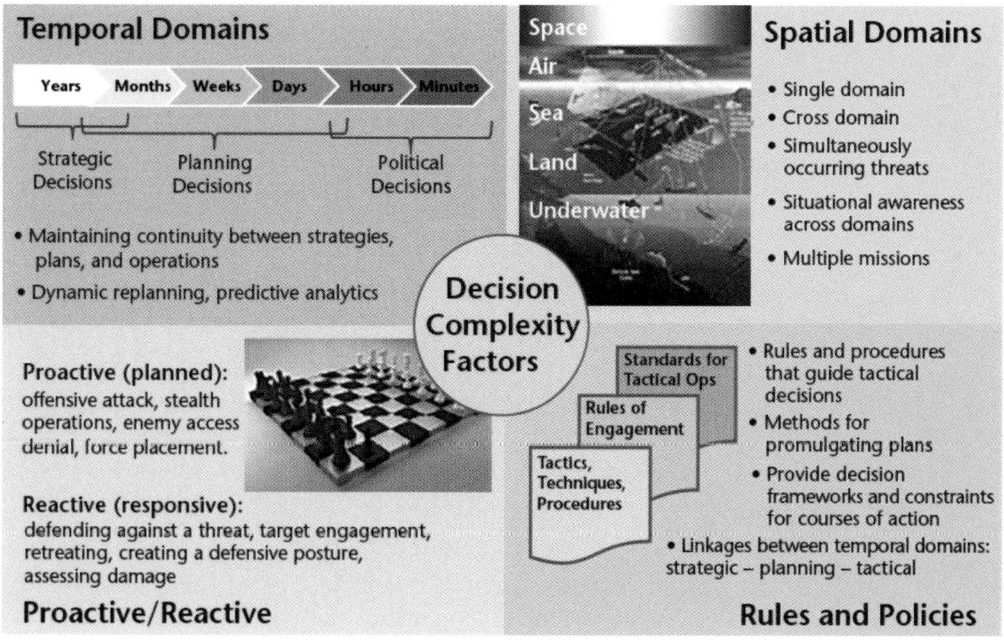

SOURCE: Reproduced from Johnson and Treadway, 2019, p. 72.

in an environment with minimal features represented. However, in complex domains, the problem of determining a "good representation" is challenging.[39] In lieu of finding a good representation, the temptation may be to create an environment that captures as much as possible, but that creates a risk that the RL will learn from correlations in data that do not tie to its learning objective.[40]

In each case, having RL interact with a simulation of the complex environments needed for the battle management scenario of Figure 1.4 can result in poor decisions. One could, however, use the simulations to bootstrap the initial learning of RL, as is done with gaming, and assume that it would learn from feedback under real-world battle conditions. The risk would likely be unacceptable to cede battle management control to a system in which one has little confidence so that it may interact with its environment and explore the consequences of its decisions. Given also that few such scenarios actually exist, the need for many training examples as shown in gaming would likely necessitate the use of simulated data in some

[39] Simon S. Du, Sham M. Kakade, Ruosong Wang, and Lin F. Yang, "Is a Good Representation Sufficient for Sample Efficient Reinforcement Learning?" arXiv preprint arXiv:1910.03016, 2019.

[40] Xingyou Song, Yiding Jiang, Stephen Tu, Yilun Du, and Behnam Neyshabur, "Observational Overfitting in Reinforcement Learning," arXiv preprint arXiv:1912.02975, 2019.

fashion, and thus the problem of simulation bias creeps back in. Chapter 2 discusses RL in autonomous driving, in which the system is trained offline for selected scenarios in which the RL fails. This method presents the same challenge for the problem shown in Figure 1.4. The system fails in a real-world situation that it did not train for in a simulated environment. Again, the challenge of how to train RL in a real-world battle scenario is present.

Transfer of Expertise from a Game to Reality

Games generally operate with rules and environments particular to the game. Generalizing play across games can be challenging because the RL algorithm overfits to the data generated in the game.[41] In other words, RL that learns to play the game becomes a specialist in the game. Domain generalization is the ability of AI to transfer learned skills across domains, and for RL it is especially difficult because of multiple domain shifts, such as visual appearance, rewards, and dynamics.[42] If we consider the domains of Figure 1.4, complexities in domains exist in environment, tactics, rules, decision times, target engagements, and many other aspects, all of which would likely differ from those of a game. The risks in this case stem from placing a specialist in one type of battle in charge of a different type.

We can use examples of transfer learning in games to illustrate potential challenges involved in transfer learning. Das et al. tested the ability of RL trained on Atari games to play other games and attempted to determine how rapidly such trained systems can learn the new game.[43] In relatively simple games (e.g., Pong), transfer learning did help in bootstrapping the learning process. In more-complex games (e.g., Space Invaders), there was negative transfer learning, in which the system performed worse as compared with training from scratch because it generalized its performance.

While these examples are between games and not between a game (or simulated environment) and reality, they do offer some insight. First, we can conclude that success in a game would not necessarily transfer well to a real-world situation in which elements of the environment (complexity, strategy, etc.) differ significantly from the game. Such is obvious, as it is akin to concluding that an expert in chess strategy, given no other experience, will likely be able to suddenly master a complex battle. A more relevant conclusion comes from the pretrained complex games. Here, pretrained games performed worse than those trained from scratch, as the RL essentially "unlearned" strategies that transferred poorly. Further, the complexity of the games used (e.g., Space Invaders) is considerably less than those that might be of interest (e.g., transferring a multiplayer game, such as Dota 2, to a battle environment). Thus,

---

[41] Karl Cobbe, Oleg Klimov, Chris Hesse, Taehoon Kim, and John Schulman, "Quantifying Generalization in Reinforcement Learning," *Proceedings of the International Conference on Machine Learning*, 2019.

[42] K. Zhou, Z. Liu, Y. Qiao, T. Xiang, and C. C. Loy, "Domain Generalization: A Survey," *IEEE Transactions on Pattern Analysis and Machine Intelligence*, Vol. 45, No. 4, 2023.

[43] A. Das, V. Shroff, A. Jain, and G. Sharma, "Knowledge Transfer Between Similar Atari Games Using Deep Q-Networks to Improve Performance," *2021 12th International Conference on Computing Communication and Networking Technologies (ICCCNT)*, 2021.

in the battle management application shown in Figure 1.4, we would likely train an RL system in a simulated environment—i.e., a game. The transferred game would be the actual battle environment, and we might expect deviations from the simulated environment to cause the RL to perform poorly, at least initially. "Poorly," in this case, is relative to the untrained RL.

It should be noted that the pretrained model would not be valueless because it could rapidly adapt to differences in reality if the simulated environment sufficiently captures reality. The nature of the problem underlies the impracticality of the situation. The training, in this case, consists of repeating thousands of actual battles in which the RL learns from its decisions. Thus, if pretrained models cannot be relied upon to perform well initially, it is unlikely that they are practical for use. The risk is unacceptable loss before one achieves a trained system.

Such a conclusion does not indicate that RL is completely unsuited for DoD applications. It simply indicates that, in situations in which a simulation cannot sufficiently capture the necessary elements of its working environment, a practical means must exist for it to train in such an environment without unacceptable risk.

Intransitivity and Strategic Depth

Game theory provides an interesting insight into game strategies that can potentially be generalized to problems of RL. An important concept in game theory is that of a *Nash equilibrium*.[44] A Nash equilibrium is a set of strategies for players in which no player can gain overall payoff by unilaterally changing strategy. A simple example exists for the game of tic-tac-toe. This is an example of a two-player, zero-sum game in which two players must not only play to win but also play to prevent the opponent from winning. The Nash equilibrium for this game is that the player with the opening move plays a corner because it has the potential to win if the opposing player does not pick the center in the following move. If the opposing player does not wish to lose, choosing the center can always result in a draw.[45] The Nash equilibrium can be generalized across other types of strategic-form games.[46]

The importance of the Nash equilibrium has been its utility in predicting the behavior of people in situations in which different incentives exist.[47] It has been especially useful in the field of economics to predict how participants can behave rationally to maximize their interests in cooperative and noncooperative situations.[48] In terms of RL, identification of Nash

[44] Charles A. Holt and Alvin E. Roth, "The Nash Equilibrium: A Perspective," *Proceedings of the National Academy of Sciences*, Vol. 101, No. 12, 2004.

[45] See "Game Theory in Tic Tac Toe," *Networks* blog, Cornell University, October 21, 2015.

[46] Asuman E. Ozdaglar, "Strategic Form Games and Nash Equilibrium," in J. Baillieul and T. Samad, eds., *Encyclopedia of Systems and Control*, Springer, 2013.

[47] Holt and Roth, 2004.

[48] Roger B. Myerson, "Nash Equilibrium and the History of Economic Theory," *Voprosy Economiki*, Vol. 6, 2010.

equilibria can be a means to study good (although not necessarily optimal) strategies within the game.[49] It may also be useful as a measure of how difficult a game is to solve.[50]

Coupled to the concept of a Nash equilibrium is that of *transitivity* in a game.[51] A *transitive game* consists of transitive strategies such that, if a strategy A is better than B, and B is better than C, then A must be better than C. If A is worse than C, then the game is intransitive. An intransitive strategy seems counterintuitive initially, but it is easy to demonstrate. The classic example of a *intransitive game* is that of rock-paper-scissors, in which rock beats scissors, scissors beats paper, and paper beats rock, leading to a cyclic strategy.[52] Cyclic strategies can be problematic for learning algorithms because they can trap them in cyclic loops.[53] Czarnecki et al. posits that many challenging games contain intransitive strategies and that the process of learning to become a professional player consists of learning such strategies, and further that such strategies explain why many such games require a population of strategies for successful training.[54] Sanjaya et al. use an open dataset of chess moves[55] and the Elo rating system[56] as a means to measure the difficulty of solving chess from its number of intransitive plays; the results support the view that the number of intransitive plays is tied to the difficulty of the game.[57]

Another useful concept in game theory is that of *strategic depth*.[58] Strategic depth relates to how many moves a strategy takes to play out. It is hypothesized that strategic depth cou-

---

49 Ann Nowé, Peter Vrancx, and Yann-Michaël De Hauwere, "Game Theory and Multi-Agent Reinforcement Learning," in M. Wiering, and M. van Otterlo, eds., *Reinforcement Learning: Adaptation, Learning, and Optimization*, Vol. 12, Springer, 2012.

50 Michael Ummels and Dominik Wojtczak, "The Complexity of Nash Equilibria in Simple Stochastic Multiplayer Games," paper presented at Automata, Languages and Programming: 36th International Colloquium, ICALP 2009, Rhodes, Greece, July 5–12, 2009.

51 Yin et al., 2021.

52 Timothy N. Cason, Daniel Friedman, and E. D. Hopkins, "Cycles and Instability in a Rock-Paper-Scissors Population Game: A Continuous Time Experiment," *Review of Economic Studies*, Vol. 81, No. 1, 2014.

53 David Balduzzi, Marta Garnelo, Yoram Bachrach, Wojciech Czarnecki, Julien Perolat, Max Jaderberg, and Thore Graepel, "Open-Ended Learning in Symmetric Zero-Sum Games," *Proceedings of the International Conference on Machine Learning*, 2019.

54 Wojciech M. Czarnecki, Gauthier Gidel, Brendan Tracey, Karl Tuyls, Shayegan Omidshafiei, David Balduzzi, and Max Jaderberg, "Real World Games Look Like Spinning Tops," *Advances in Neural Information Processing Systems*, Vol. 33, 2020.

55 Lichess, homepage, undated.

56 The Elo rating system is a measure of a chess player's performance; see Mark E. Glickman and Albyn C. Jones, "Rating the Chess Rating System," Boston University, 1999.

57 Ricky Sanjaya, Jun Wang, and Yaodong Yang, "Measuring the Non-Transitivity in Chess," *Algorithms*, Vol. 15, No. 5, 2022.

58 Frank Lantz, Aaron Isaksen, Alexander Jaffe, Andy Nealen, and Julian Togelius, *Depth in Strategic Games*, Association for the Advancement of Artificial Intelligence, 2017; Matthew Stephenson, Diego

pled with complexity in games correlates to the learning challenge and associated interest from players. Both Go and chess, for example, have strategies of high depth and complexity, resulting in progressive learning and consequent interest from their followers.

While strategic depth is not tied to the transitive nature of the game, linking them may be useful to do in the consideration of DoD applications. Consider again the battle management domains of Figure 1.4. A system must be able to cope with a range of temporal domains, depending on the size and complexity of the battle space. A mixture of tactics may be in play simultaneously over the battle space, some of which may have strategic depths lasting minutes to, potentially, weeks or years. Dynamics of the battle may change objectives as the battle unfolds. Intransitivities may exist between the tactics, rules of engagement, and objectives of the Blue team versus those of the Red team.[59]

Thus, while the complexity of a battle management system as indicated by the complex domains shown in Figure 1.4 might be impossible to quantify, the system may give general indications why it might be too challenging for an RL algorithm, at least from use in gaming. Such an algorithm, to be successful, would likely have to learn a large range of diverse strategies of varying strategic depth and combinations of transitivity and intransitivity. Such strategies would be multiplayer, especially in large theaters of operation. Generality would be required because there is no guarantee that the battle the system trained under is the same as the one fought. To use a system other than one trained under such conditions would risk having a system that makes decisions with unacceptable losses while it learns how to conduct a battle effectively.

Conclusions

RL is a powerful algorithmic tool that has demonstrated great success within the field of gaming. Within this field, RL has solved games of strategy with increasing complexity. Such success may not transfer well to DoD problems involving tactical or strategic decisionmaking. Such a system would have complexities that exceed those of current games. Further, the characteristics of games, such as limited or fixed rules and simplified or differing environments, do not lend themselves to the complexities or generalities needed in such DoD systems.

Perez-Liebana, Mark Nelson, Ahmed Khalifa, and Alexander Zook, "Game Complexity vs Strategic Depth," matthewstephenson.info, 2019.

[59] Transitive choice is tied to perceived rationality. An irrational actor may contribute to intransitivity. See Maya Bar-Hillel and Avishai Margalit, "How Vicious Are Cycles of Intransitive Choice?" *Theory and Decision*, Vol. 24, 1988.

CHAPTER 2

Further Technical Challenges of RL in Broader Problems

This chapter explores some of the technical challenges of RL as it is applied to broader problems, such as might be encountered in DoD applications. Some of the risk factors of RL come from experiences with other forms of AI, such as resource constraints or misaligned organizational expectations. Such risks are common to many complex software projects, and RL is not likely to be immune to them. Other challenges can arise from the complexity of the problem itself: problems in sufficient simulation and training coverage or unexpected shifts between training and operational use. Finally, the example of autonomous driving is used as an example of real-world applications using RL in some form. While published data are scarce, they do provide useful insights on using RL in real-world situations.

Failure in RL Systems

To consider the risk of failure in RL systems, it is useful to look to industry at the deployment of AI systems and the factors that have caused them to fail. Westenberger, Schuler, and Schlegel collected input from experts in different industries and positions with expertise in AI.[1] Categories and factors contributing to the failure of AI projects are shown in Table 2.1.

While our study did not focus on applications involving RL, the categories and factors relating to failure in its use are expected to be shared with those identified in Table 2.1. Some of the risk factors relating to the technical aspects of RL are explored in this chapter. Some of the risk factors relating to use cases and organizational aspects are identified in Chapter 4, drawing on the DoD use cases discussed in Chapter 3. Factors can be interrelated (e.g., thinking too big in relation to budget), so that they might appear in different categories. This chapter mainly focuses on risk factors related to the RL technology itself.

Determining a comprehensive list of technical risk factors is challenging, given the sheer volume of literature created on the subject. In 2015, Henderson et al. estimated that close to

1 Jens Westenberger, Kajetan Schuler, and Dennis Schlegel, "Failure of AI Projects: Understanding the Critical Factors," *Procedia Computer Science*, Vol. 196, 2022.

TABLE 2.1
Risk Categories and Risk Factors in AI Failure

Risk Category	Risk Factor
Unrealistic expectations	Misunderstanding of AI capabilities
	Thinking too big
Use case related issues	Missing value or cost-benefit ratio
	Complexity
	Low error tolerance
Organizational constraints	Budget too low
	Regulations
Lack of key resources	Lack of employees with expertise
	Data availability
Technological issues	Model instability
	Lack of transparency (black box problem)
	Possible result manipulation

SOURCE: Reproduced from Westenberger, Schuler, and Schlegel, 2022.

15,000 papers were devoted to the subject of RL, with a continual rise since 1990.[2] Such a volume of research, the ad hoc nature of algorithm development, and the lack of an analytical basis for ML behavior make a thorough analysis of the RL challenges difficult. Fortunately, papers by Dulac-Arnold et al.,[3] Williams and Yampolskiy,[4] Amodei et al.,[5] and Kumar et al.[6] summarize a range of challenges in RL that may be classified as *grand challenges*. These challenges give rise to failure modes within RL, and they serve as a means to identify technical risk factors. Although our literature reviews have produced a range of papers addressing

2 Peter Henderson, Riashat Islam, Philip Bachman, Joelle Pineau, Doina Precup, and David Meger, "Deep Reinforcement Learning That Matters," paper presented at Thirty-Second Association for the Advancement of Artificial Intelligence Conference on Artificial Intelligence (AAAI-18), New Orleans, Louisiana, February 2–7, 2018.

3 Gabriel Dulac-Arnold, Nir Levine, Daniel J. Mankowitz, Jerry Li, Cosmin Paduraru, Sven Gowal, and Todd Hester, "Challenges of Real-World Reinforcement Learning: Definitions, Benchmarks and Analysis," *Machine Learning*, Vol. 110, No. 9, 2021.

4 Robert Williams and Roman Yampolskiy, "Understanding and Avoiding AI Failures: A Practical Guide," *Philosophies*, Vol. 6, No. 3, 2021.

5 Dario Amodei, Chris Olah, Jacob Steinhardt, Paul Christiano, John Schulman, and Dan Mané, "Concrete Problems in AI Safety," arXiv preprint arXiv:1606.06565, 2016.

6 Ram Shankar Siva Kumar, David O. Brien, Kendra Albert, Salomé Viljöen, and Jeffrey Snover, "Failure Modes in Machine Learning Systems," arXiv preprint arXiv:1911.11034, 2019.

each, again, the empirical nature of the field can result in solutions that seem to work in certain applications with no confidence that the solutions generalize. For example, Amodei et al. list one challenge as "robustness to distributional shift."[7] This challenge is related to the RL agent responding as expected when the environment changes. A survey paper by Padakandla uses the terminology "dynamically varying environments" and presents a wide range of approaches for different applications, using different types of RL, with various advantages and disadvantages.[8] This discussion does not apply just to one challenge, but it appears to apply to all. Indeed, Dulac-Arnold et al. discuss the same observation but, importantly, point out the lack of research addressing *all* such challenges simultaneously.[9]

Lack of Domain Generalization

Domain generalization is a concept in AI in which a system properly functions in a domain different from the one in which it was trained.[10] The assumption is that the statistical distribution of the domain in which the AI is trained is identical to the one in which it is expected to operate. If not, then the assumption that the trained AI has converged on a correct solution is no longer valid, and its behavior may diverge from what was intended in training. In other words, the statistical distribution of trained domain has *shifted* from that of the operational domain. RL is especially prone to distributional shift because it has not only a spatial component but also a temporal one.[11] In a real-world operational setting, additional complexities arise from uncertainties. RL functioning correctly within a range of domains is considered *robust*, and it is an active field of study.[12]

Domain Size and Computational Feasibility

As discussed in Chapter 1, the challenge of gaming was tied to several aspects of the game complexity, including state space, the number of players, whether the game has a stochastic element, and the number and depth of transitive and intransitive plays. These can be loosely thought of as the *domain size* of the problem, estimates of which can become very challenging

---

[7] Amodei et al., 2016.

[8] Sindhu Padakandla, "A Survey of Reinforcement Learning Algorithms for Dynamically Varying Environments," *ACM Computing Surveys*, Vol. 54, No. 6, 2021.

[9] Dulac-Arnold et al., 2021.

[10] Zhou et al., 2023; Amodei et al., 2016.

[11] Padakandla, 2021.

[12] Janosch Moos, Kay Hansel, Hany Abdulsamad, Svenja Stark, Debora Clever, and Jan Peters, "Robust Reinforcement Learning: A Review of Foundations and Recent Advances," *Machine Learning and Knowledge Extraction*, Vol. 4, No. 1, 2022.

as the various aspects of this space grow. As the domain size grows, however, we can expect that the need for computation will grow as well. If we use the game Dota 2 as an example,[13] the computation required by RL to solve the game was reported as 770 petaflops per second (/s)[14] performed over ten months. In comparison, the current supercomputer clocks in at 1,600 petaflops/s.[15]

OpenAI provides a chart showing the progress of AI with respect to benchmarks over time and an estimate of the total computation needed for each. It is shown in Figure 2.1.

As shown, beginning in approximately 2012, AI computing needs began to sharply rise as ML models based on deep neural networks (DNNs) began to rise in prominence. DNNs provide the power to make complex inferences in many of the most significant milestones in the different types of ML models, including those of RL. Before 2012, computational power needed for AI models roughly tracked the two-year doubling known as Moore's law. This

FIGURE 2.1

A Plot of Computing Power Needed over Time for AI

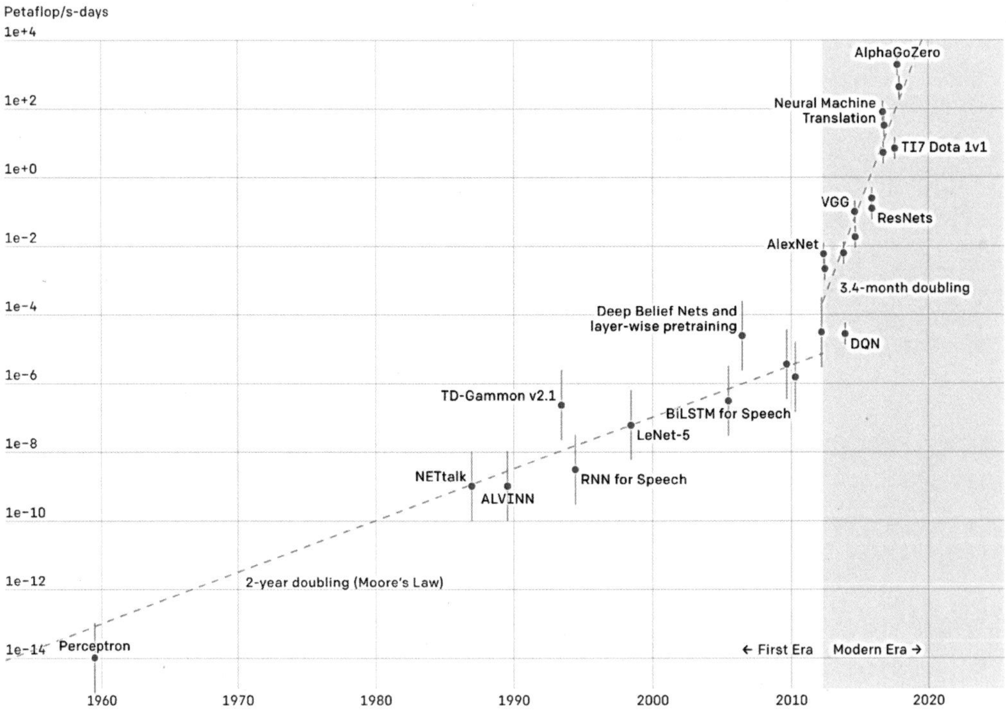

SOURCE: Reproduced from Dario Amodei and Danny Hernandez, "AI and Compute," webpage, OpenAI, May 16, 2018.

---

[13] Berner et al., 2019.

[14] Petaflops per second is a measure of computational speed (peta = 10^{15}).

[15] Oak Ridge National Laboratory, "Frontier: Direction of Discovery," webpage, U.S. Department of Energy, undated.

trend tracks the progress of generalized computing as represented by a single-package microprocessor. Moore's law increases come essentially free, in the sense that additional computing does not cost in terms of increases in power consumption or expense. Increases in computational power beyond that tracked by Moore's law do cost, however, and significantly, in terms of the growing computational needs of AI. Consider that the computation needed for ML began to double *every 3.4 months* after 2012 (Figure 2.1), far outstripping the "free lunch" provided by Moore's law.

This computational complexity has several impacts, one of which is energy usage. Energy usage data for large-scale RL algorithms are difficult to estimate because of the lack of detailed reporting in the literature of these data. In general, energy estimations of supervised ML algorithms, such as natural language processing, are available from the work of several authors.[16] We will draw from Patterson et al., who estimated the power usage for several large ML models having a deep learning (DL) architecture called *transformers*,[17] which are suited for RL applications.[18] Since the calculations are based on hardware applicable across different DL applications, it is assumed that power draw will be roughly the same across algorithms when using the same number of processors. Table 2.2 summarizes the resulting power draw as the size of the ML model changes.

The total energy required to train large-scale models can be quite substantial. For example, the Neural Architecture Search (NAS) model shown in the first column was estimated to take 7.5 megawatt-hours (MWh), approximately the average retail electrical demand of 11 consumers over one month; the larger GPT-3 model was estimated to take 1,287 MWh to train, about enough to supply the demand of a small city of 20,000 residential consumers in one month.[19] Beyond training a large DL model, running a trained model incurs additional

[16] N. C. Thompson, K. Greenewald, K. Lee, and G. F. Manso, "Deep Learning's Diminishing Returns: The Cost of Improvement Is Becoming Unsustainable," *IEEE Spectrum*, Vol. 58, No. 10, 2021; Alexandra Sasha Luccioni, Sylvain Viguier, and Anne-Laure Ligozat, "Estimating the Carbon Footprint of BLOOM, a 176B Parameter Language Model," arXiv preprint arXiv:2211.02001, 2022; Radosvet Desislavov, Fernando Martínez-Plumed, and José Hernández-Orallo, "Compute and Energy Consumption Trends in Deep Learning Inference," arXiv preprint arXiv:2109.05472, 2021; Sadasivan Shankar and Albert Reuther, "Trends in Energy Estimates for Computing in AI/Machine Learning Accelerators, Supercomputers, and Compute-Intensive Applications," *Proceedings of the IEEE High Performance Extreme Computing Conference (HPEC)*, 2022.

[17] David Patterson, Joseph Gonzalez, Quoc Le, Chen Liang, Lluis-Miquel Munguia, Daniel Rothchild, David So, Maud Texier, and Jeff Dean, "Carbon Emissions and Large Neural Network Training," arXiv preprint arXiv:2104.10350, 2021.

[18] William Fedus, Jeff Dean, and Barret Zoph, "A Review of Sparse Expert Models in Deep Learning," arXiv preprint arXiv:2209.01667, 2022; Lili Chen, Kevin Lu, Aravind Rajeswaran, Kimin Lee, Aditya Grover, Misha Laskin, Pieter Abbeel, Aravind Srinivas, and Igor Mordatch, "Decision Transformer: Reinforcement Learning via Sequence Modeling," *Advances in Neural Information Processing Systems*, Vol. 34, 2021.

[19] Data are drawn from the U.S. Energy Information Administration's EIA-861 schedules 4A and 4D and EIA-861S for the year 2021 (U.S. Energy Information Administration, *Annual Electric Power Industry Report*, EIA-861, 2021). Estimated retail consumer electrical demand of 0.65 MWh/month was used in the calculations.

TABLE 2.2
Power Estimations of Several Large DL Models

Technology	Evolved Transformer (NAS)	T5	Meena	Gshard-600B	Switch Transformer	GPT-3
Date of run	December 2018	September 2019	December 2019	April 2020	October 2020	2020
Measured performance (TFLOPS/s)[a]	24.8	45.6	42.3	48	34.4	24.6
Days to train	6.8	20	30	3.1	27	14.8
Total Computation to train (zetaflops)[b]	2.91	40.5	112	13.3	82.2	314
Total energy consumed to train (MWh)	7.5	85.7	232	24.1	179	1,287
Processor	TPU v2	TPU v3	TPU v3	TPU v3	TPU v3	V100 GPU
Average power (W)	221	283	283	283	283	325
Number of processors	200	512	1,024	1,024	1,024	10,000
Estimated run energy (kW)[c]	44.2	145	290	290	290	3,250

SOURCE: Features data from Patterson et al., 2021.

NOTE: GPU = graphics processing unit; kW = kilowatt; TPU = tensor processing unit; W = watt.

[a] TFLOPS = 10^{12} floating point operations/s.

[b] Zetaflops = 10^{21} floating point operations/s.

[c] Run energy is derived from multiplying average processor power by number of processors.

costs. As per the power usage of the GPT-3 model shown in Table 2.2, the net energy to run the model is approximately 3.25 megawatts (MW), the average residential electrical demand of approximately 13,000 consumers.[20]

Another factor that weighs on the practicality of training and running a large-scale DoD application using RL is the data requirements of such a model. Ivanov et al. found that one of the key bottlenecks in training the transformer models (used in the data of Table 2.2) is data movement.[21] That analysis refers to data movement within the hardware accelerators, but Zhou, Yi, and Zhang point out that 70 percent of the total model execution time can be spent migrating data back and forth between the hardware accelerators and memory stor-

[20] EIA-861, 2021, data based on the utility Volt Electricity, in Houston, Texas, with a reported electrical demand of 3.37 MW over 13,542 customers (U.S. Energy Information Administration, 2021).

[21] Andrei Ivanov, Nikoli Dryden, Tal Ben-Nun, Shigang Li, and Torsten Hoefler, "Data Movement Is All You Need: A Case Study on Optimizing Transformers," *Proceedings of Machine Learning and Systems*, Vol. 3, 2021.

age.[22] Such impediments to using a large-scale model would likely be a limiting factor in a complex DoD problem with data flowing from sources external to the RL model. In the tactical battle management system of Figure 1.4, data from several complex domains would need to be used as inputs for the system. These data would likely need to be simulated in some fashion during training, but, in real-time usage, the data would be provided from the physical environment for the RL to make real-time decisions. Collection of data dispersed across domains (e.g., intelligence data, environmental data, logistics data) would present challenges in terms of data concurrency (e.g., delays in data collection), data uncertainty (e.g., from data noise or dropouts), and even data network bandwidth for large, continuous data input.

Regarding the risk categories listed for failure in AI projects, large RL models cover several areas in terms of complexity, data availability, and even "thinking too big." Further, the electrical demands for such a model may make an expected return on investment less competitive than other ways of accomplishing the same mission.

Explainability and Trust

A DNN represents a complex set of interconnected nodes that process input data to make decisions. There is a fundamental challenge in explaining how the DNNs make these decisions given their black box nature.[23] The risk in such systems is that the output of such systems might be ignored or dismissed, even if such a system outperforms humans, as reported by Polonski.[24] He studied Watson for Oncology, an ML-based decision tool for oncology;[25] physicians using this tool viewed it as redundant when it confirmed their diagnoses and viewed it with suspicion otherwise. Overall, the effort was deemed a failure,[26] even though a metastudy confirmed its value as a diagnostic tool to supplement physician diagnoses.[27] Interestingly, the metastudy measured comparison between recommendations of Watson

[22] Zixuan Zhou, Shushu Yi, and Jie Zhang, "Survey on Storage-Accelerator Data Movement," *CCF Transactions on High Performance Computing*, Vol. 4, 2022.

[23] F. K. Došilović, M. Brčić, and N. Hlupić, "Explainable Artificial Intelligence: A Survey," *Proceedings of the 2018 41st International Convention on Information and Communication Technology, Electronics and Microelectronics (MIPRO)*, 2018.

[24] Vyacheslav Polonski, "People Don't Trust AI—Here's How We Can Change That," *Scientific American*, Vol. 10, 2018.

[25] S. P. Somashekhar, Martín-J. Sepúlveda, Andrew D. Norden, Amit Rauthan, Kumar Arun, Poonam Patil, Ramya Y. Ethadka, and Rohit C. Kumar, "Early Experience with IBM Watson for Oncology (WFO) Cognitive Computing System for Lung and Colorectal Cancer Treatment," *Journal of Clinical Oncology*, Vol. 35, No. 15, Supp., 2017.

[26] Eliza Strickland, "IBM Watson, Heal Thyself: How IBM Overpromised and Underdelivered on AI Health Care," *IEEE Spectrum*, Vol. 56, No. 4, 2019.

[27] Zhou Jie, Zeng Zhiying, and Li Li, "A Meta-Analysis of Watson for Oncology in Clinical Application," *Scientific Reports*, Vol. 11, No. 1, March 11, 2021.

and diagnostic teams. Had Watson consistently showed concordance with such teams, presumably trust in the system could develop to where its use as a tool would progress to acceptance of it. Distrust of the system created a vulnerability of acceptance and use. Such has been the case with several such tools, as reported by Strickland.[28]

Another potential risk stemming from lack of explainability is that of the human tendency to anthropomorphize AI.[29] *Anthropomorphizing* may cause a user to assume some common motivation or thought process that may cloud the proper evaluation of the AI's behavior. *Confirmation bias*,[30] which tends to give data confirming our own assumptions greater weight, may also cause risk. If a user is monitoring the behavior of an AI system, assuming that a confirming decision extrapolates to general model correctness may lead to unwarranted trust in the AI system. Further monitoring may, in this case, lead to ignoring signs of a malfunctioning system.

Statistical measures that could accurately predict failure rates in RL are challenging for large models. Running the model to gather statistical measures of failure assumes that the data used as inputs are statistically representational. As discussed earlier, if the input changes—for example, through a change in the model environment—assumptions on the input data distribution may no longer be valid. Even with board games, the state space complexity grows in state space size to where the full space is intractably large to compute (see Table 1.1). Larger models, with multiple domains of complexity as might be expected in the battle management system of Figure 1.4, would likely be intractable for a brute force statistical approach.

Reward Function

One risk of RL derives from its use of a *reward function* to train the agent. The reward function must provide feedback to the agent such that it reaches the ultimate goal of the application while allowing the agent to explore the problem domain sufficiently in the process. An agent that randomly explores with too little feedback may become computationally intractable, especially as the size of the problem grows. Conversely, leading the agent along a solution path with too-frequent rewards may not allow the agent to learn the problem space sufficiently and cause failure in an actual application. The problem of setting up the RL agent to efficiently explore the problem space in real-world situations is a challenge that grows with the size of the problem. Unfortunately, constructing the reward function that results in sufficient exploration can be difficult, and a poor design might result in unwanted behavior—

[28] Strickland, 2019.

[29] Arleen Salles, Kathinka Evers, and Michele Farisco, "Anthropomorphism in AI," *AJOB Neuroscience*, Vol. 11, No. 2, 2020.

[30] Ramya Srinivasan and Ajay Chander, "Biases in AI Systems," *Communications of the ACM*, Vol. 64, No. 8, 2021.

such as constantly repeating an action that results in a reward with no incentive to explore further.[31]

A poorly designed reward function can result in a phenomenon called *reward hacking*.[32] Reward hacking is when an agent is rewarded for achieving goals not intended by the designer. For example, a designer wishes to create an RL-controlled race car that competes on a circular track. The RL agent is rewarded every time the car races past the finish line but penalized for crashing into another car or the walls of the track. During training, the agent discovers that, if it races in a circle around the finish line, it can cross the finish line repeatedly without circumnavigating the track. Thus, the agent becomes stuck in a circular loop not intended by the designer.

Reward hacking can manifest in different ways, the number of which can grow with problem complexity.[33] In a DoD system, for example, an agent rewarded for target kills may result in friendly fire in a poorly designed system.[34] Other such unsafe behavior can arise simply from the exploratory process of an agent—for example, when a robot agent might run into objects as it discovers the limits of the environment. Such behavior may be fine in a simulated environment, but it could be intolerable in a real one. As problem sizes and complexity grow, safe exploration becomes more difficult to ensure.[35] Ensuring safety in RL is an outstanding problem with a range of approaches under study.[36]

Any RL-based DoD system must ensure that unanticipated behavior does not result in unacceptable consequences through reward hacking or unsafe operation. Specifying a reward function and placing limits on unsafe behavior may become untenable if broad missions have ill-defined goals and unanticipated variables. For example, a commander may have a clear understanding of what a successful mission would look like, but implicit in this understanding are assumptions that may be difficult for a designer to completely specify to properly train an RL system. Multiple missions might involve different objectives, such as transporting war refugees while defeating an enemy. Designing an RL system to execute such missions might result in unforeseen side effects, such as sinking a ship carrying civilians to clear a path to an enemy target.

---

[31] Pawel Ladosz, Lilian Weng, Minwoo Kim, and Hyondong Oh, "Exploration in Deep Reinforcement Learning: A Survey," *Information Fusion*, Vol. 85, September 2022.

[32] Amodei et al., 2016.

[33] Sina Yaghoobzadehtari, Colin Owusu Adomako, and Siavash Paidar, "Elaborate Operational Requirements to Address Reward Hacking in Reinforcement Learning Agents," thesis, Chalmers University of Technology and University of Gothenberg, 2019.

[34] Williams and Yampolskiy, 2021.

[35] Ladosz et al., 2022.

[36] Javier Garcia and Fernando Fernández, "A Comprehensive Survey on Safe Reinforcement Learning," *Journal of Machine Learning Research*, Vol. 16, No. 1, 2015; Mattijs Baert, Sam Leroux, and Pieter Simoens, "Inverse Reinforcement Learning Through Logic Constraint Inference," *Machine Learning*, Vol. 112, 2023.

Vulnerability to Adversarial Attacks

DNNs are known for exhibiting unusual vulnerabilities in which small changes to input data result in large changes in output.[37] These examples are called *adversarial* because an adversary wanting to cause a DNN to misbehave could exploit them. Since their discovery, such vulnerabilities have been widely studied, with some claiming that they are not "bugs" but features of DNNs.[38] Others have claimed that they may be inevitable.[39] Since RL agents might have DNNs as their core learning system, it is not surprising that these agents can also be subject to adversarial exploitation in different ways. An interesting example is given in video form on GitHub.[40] Two RL-trained agents are playing a game in which one player (Blue) attempts to pass the other (Red). Normally, you would expect the Red agent to behave as a human and block or tackle the Blue agent to prevent the Blue agent from passing. Such behavior is present, but an odd (adversarial) example is shown. The Red agent suddenly falls and flails about on the ground. The Blue agent, not having seen such a behavior, collapses. Instead of simply exploiting the opportunity to pass the Red player flailing on the ground as a human might, the Blue player fails catastrophically. While Red and Blue agents can mutually train against one another to reduce such weaknesses in a process called *adversarial machine learning*,[41] it is not clear that all such weaknesses can be found, especially in a complex, broad application in which thorough computational exploration may be infeasible.[42] While any adversarial weakness may result in system risk, especially troubling would be those that might be general in nature and used by an adversary during a mission. If multiple RL systems carry such weaknesses, an attack might result in unacceptably high cost that is broad in impact. Missions covered by broad RL systems might suffer coverage challenges if a system needs to be taken offline and retrained to mitigate such vulnerability, resulting in mission failure.

---

[37] Christian Szegedy, Wojciech Zaremba, Ilya Sutskever, Joan Bruna, Dumitru Erhan, Ian J. Goodfellow, and Rob Fergus, "Intriguing Properties of Neural Networks," arXiv preprint arXiv:1312.6199, 2014.

[38] Andrew Ilyas, Shibani Santurkar, Dimitris Tsipras, Logan Engstrom, Brandon Tran, and Aleksander Madry, "Adversarial Examples Are Not Bugs, They Are Features," *Advances in Neural Information Processing Systems*, Vol. 32, 2019.

[39] Ali Shafahi, W. Ronny Huang, Christoph Studer, Soheil Feizi, and Tom Goldstein, "Are Adversarial Examples Inevitable?" paper presented at the Seventh International Conference on Learning Representations, May 7, 2019; Adam Gleave, Michael Dennis, Cody Wild, Neel Kant, Sergey Levine, and Stuart Russell, "Adversarial Policies," webpage, GitHub, undated.

[40] Gleave et al., undated.

[41] Battista Biggio and Fabio Roli, "Wild Patterns: Ten Years After the Rise of Adversarial Machine Learning," *Pattern Recognition*, Vol. 84, December 1, 2018.

[42] I. Ilahi, M. Usama, J. Qadir, M. U. Janjua, A. Al-Fuqaha, D. T. Hoang, and D. Niyato, "Challenges and Countermeasures for Adversarial Attacks on Deep Reinforcement Learning," *IEEE Transactions on Artificial Intelligence*, Vol. 3, No. 2, 2022.

Imitation Learning, Offline Training, and Retraining

One of the concerns regarding RL in real-world settings has been the need for the agent to interact with the environment to learn. The high number of interactions needed for learning, coupled with the potential for unsafe behavior, can make real-world interaction untenable. Thus, simulated environments are the default means to allow an RL agent sufficient latitude to explore both in safety and in a reasonable time for the potentially millions of interactions needed for learning.

Another means of training is to use data collected from existing live interaction through imitation learning (IL).[43] This type of learning is useful when there are many examples of expert interactions that can be essentially imitated by the RL agent. When examples are suboptimal (i.e., not demonstrated by experts) or noisy, offline training performs better.[44] Offline reinforcement learning (ORL) allows an agent to be trained using example data, but it still tries to devise an optimal policy to perform the demonstrated action.[45] An example of the application of such learning is autonomous driving,[46] in which data can be collected by following existing drivers.

IL and ORL have the potential to reduce simulated data, but they can do so only if the agent has access to many real-world examples. Data storage can also be problematic if data collection and training are not simultaneous. Further, both can suffer from distributional shift if differences exist between the example data and what the RL agent encounters in operation. There are ways to improve robustness of the learning agent to such differences,[47] but these likely cannot anticipate large deviations from collected examples. For DoD examples, learning behavior from repeated missions, such as the movement of cargo or logistics, could be appropriate examples for IL or ORL.

Once an RL agent is trained, it will likely encounter situations that its training does not cover. The result can range from acceptable deviations from expected behavior to behavior that has unacceptably high negative consequences. Such behavior can arise, for example,

---

[43] Ahmed Hussein, Mohamed Medhat Gaber, Eyad Elyan, and Chrisina Jayne, "Imitation Learning: A Survey of Learning Methods," *ACM Computing Surveys*, Vol. 50, No. 2, 2017.

[44] Aviral Kumar, Joey Hong, Anikait Singh, and Sergey Levine, "When Should We Prefer Offline Reinforcement Learning over Behavioral Cloning?" arXiv preprint arXiv:2204.05618, 2022.

[45] Sergey Levine, Aviral Kumar, George Tucker, and Justin Fu, "Offline Reinforcement Learning: Tutorial, Review, and Perspectives on Open Problems," arXiv preprint arXiv:2005.01643, 2020; Rafael Figueiredo Prudencio, Marcos R. O. A. Maximo, and Esther Luna Colombini, "A Survey on Offline Reinforcement Learning: Taxonomy, Review, and Open Problems," arXiv preprint arXiv:2203.01387, 2022.

[46] Z. Zhu and H. Zhao, "A Survey of Deep RL and IL for Autonomous Driving Policy Learning," *IEEE Transactions on Intelligent Transportation Systems*, Vol. 23, No. 9, 2022; Luc Le Mero, Dewei Yi, Mehrdad Dianati, and Alexandros Mouzakitis, "A Survey on Imitation Learning Techniques for End-to-End Autonomous Vehicles," *IEEE Transactions on Intelligent Transportation Systems*, Vol. 23, No. 9, September 2022.

[47] Rui Yang, Chenjia Bai, Xiaoteng Ma, Zhaoran Wang, Chongjie Zhang, and Lei Han, "RORL: Robust Offline Reinforcement Learning via Conservative Smoothing," arXiv preprint arXiv:2206.02829, 2022.

from environmental shifts not anticipated or even from deliberate adversarial attacks. At some point, a decision must be made to retrain the RL to account for such examples. Given the high computational and time requirements of full retraining, training methods such as IL or ORL may be useful to minimize the time from a malfunctioning system to a retrained system. Such an approach would use the observed problematic situation and train around such a case.

Retraining poses several potential risks. A system whose failure is of little consequence might continue to operate while retraining occurs, especially if the risk of losing its capabilities is greater than the risk it is creating. Should any failure be of high consequence, there may be no choice but to take the system offline. In such cases, training around the failure cases may be an option—but such cases may be problematic in at least two ways. The first is that the problematic case has not been anticipated, and thus generation of training examples may be difficult to complete in time to prevent further negative consequences, should systems remain functional. Second, such examples may differ in distribution from those used to form the existing policy and cause corruption in this policy.[48] The risk in this case is that the system trained offline may no longer function as expected. Performing a complete recertification in this case before bringing the system back online may be infeasible. Thus, unless mitigation approaches are in place for handling such cases, a failure mode may become a critical problem.

Autonomous Driving

Among the applications found using RL in real-world settings, autonomous driving appeared to be the most relevant for drawing lessons for DoD. The application is attractive in that simulated driving environments are computationally tractable, and collection of large datasets is feasible from people driving in various road situations and conditions. The goal of traveling from one point to another is a clearly expressible goal. The application would provide strong advantages over manual driving, and no viable competing technology yet exists. It is a narrow application in many respects, although a functional system would need to operate in variable environments and do so safely under unpredictable conditions. Such challenges, however, would likely exist in almost any real-world DoD system of logistics, transport, and route planning.

From approximately 22 different cases of autonomous driving found, only six indicated that RL was being used in some fashion. These are listed in Table 2.3.

[48] Ruosong Wang, Yifan Wu, Ruslan Salakhutdinov, and Sham Kakade, "Instabilities of Offline RL with Pre-Trained Neural Representation," *Proceedings of the International Conference on Machine Learning*, 2021.

TABLE 2.3
Examples of Commercial Applications Using Some Form of RL

Company	Application	Location(s)	Time Frame	RL Purpose
Waymo Via[a]	Delivery transport	Arizona, California, Georgia, Texas, New Mexico	Pilot tests	IL, planning
Waymo One[b]	Taxi service	Arizona, California, New York City	Fully driverless January 2021 (Phoenix) Pilot test 2021 (San Francisco) Mapping New York 2021	IL, planning
Nuro[c]	Delivery service	Texas		Trajectory planning, behavior and motion prediction
Mobileye (Intel[d])	Taxi service	Germany		Establishing driving policy for autonomous driving
Voyage[e]	Self-driving car simulator			Steering angle prediction
Aptiv[f]	Varies from component selection to a taxi service	Across the United States, Boston, Las Vegas, Pittsburgh, Singapore	2014, 2017, present	Path planning and obstacle avoidance

[a] Tekedra Mawakana, "Partnering with UPS to Deliver on Our Mission," *Waypoint* blog, Waymo, January 29, 2020; Waymo, "Same Driver, Different Vehicle: Bringing Waymo Self-Driving Technology to Trucks," *Waypoint* blog, March 9, 2018; Waymo, "Waymo Via Is Working with J.B. Hunt to Carry Freight Across Texas," *Waypoint* blog, June 10, 2021a; Chris Brown, "Waymo Outlines Plans to Integrate Autonomous Trucking in Fleets," *Fleet Forward*, July 14, 2020.

[b] Eric Walz, "Waymo Is Deploying Its Self-Driving Vehicles in New York City," *FutureCar*, December 10, 2021.

[c] Nuro, "Find a Career That Delivers," webpage, undated.

[d] Tom Warren, "Intel Acquiring Mobileye's Self-Driving Car Technology in $15 Billion Deal," *The Verge*, March 13, 2017.

[e] Carnegie Mellon University Audiovisual Center, "Research Themes," webpage, Carnegie Mellon University Robotics Institute, undated.

[f] Aptiv, "Autonomous Mobility," webpage, undated; Niclas Carlström, "Enhancement of Radar Tracking with Low Level Radar Data," briefing slides, Aptiv, November 2019.

Waymo

Waymo is a subsidiary of Alphabet Inc. developing self-driving vehicles for taxi services and delivery transport. At the start of January 2021, Waymo began offering a fully driverless taxi service in Arizona. This service is open to the public and operates in designated areas. Waymo is currently mapping a designated portion of New York City for an eventual pilot test in the area. Waymo is also performing pilot tests in San Francisco for taxi services.

Prior to providing a taxi service to the public, (human-driven) Waymo vehicles drive repeatedly throughout a designated area to develop a map of the routes and to record real-world events for later use in training the Waymo Driver system. Completion of the mapping process is an initial step prior to the integration of real-time sensor data on the map. ML is used to identify and classify objects detected. Waymo's Perception system uses neural nets that learn to recognize objects and associate them with expected behaviors. Examples include pedestrians, vegetation, and traffic lights.[49] Waymo's Perception system is built on a decade-long data-gathering effort in collaboration with Google Research. The system uses Google's data catalog and algorithms capable of searching image labels to associate the items identified by the Waymo Driver system. In this way, the previously catalogued image data assists the Driver system with identifying encountered objects and analyzing their potential behaviors.

The data collected via the Driver system are indexed and used for training of the Perception system. The company uses IL developed by Latent Logic.[50] IL processes real-world data for training purposes. RL comes with the risk of reward maximization that is not aligned with the intent of the programmer. Recognizing this implementation limitation, the company mitigates the risk by supervising the training process and explicitly identifying to the machine the good behavior. Thus, the training benefits from human guidance with the intent of teaching the machine to behave like a human and not simply a program maximizing a reward.

As it reported in a 2019 blog post, Waymo found that learning from good situations is easier done than from bad situations.[51] Good situations, such as driving in lanes, responding to traffic lights, and turning, are numerous. Bad situations, such as accidents, have smaller datasets. In other words, there is a dataset bias toward the good situations. The lack of training data means that the machine does not have information to imitate and will not know how to respond during a collision. Even good situations with significant perturbations can challenge the response of the machine if there is a lack of training data for that situation. With these training data limitations in mind, Waymo imitates the good situations but synthesizes bad situations for training purposes. For example, the synthesized data can be based on a good situation but with a perturbation imposed. Image datasets can also be augmented with the creation of image transformations of two-dimensional camera-captured and three-dimensional light detection and ranging (LIDAR)-captured data.[52] The use of IL and model-

---

[49] James Guo, Ed Walker, and Congcong Li, "Seeing Is Knowing: Advances in Search and Image Recognition Train Waymo's Self-Driving Technology for Any Encounter," *Waypoint* blog, Waymo, February 6, 2020.

[50] Liane Yvkoff, "With Acquisition of Latent Logic, Waymo Adds Imitation Learning to Self-Driving Training," *Forbes*, December 12, 2019.

[51] Mayank Bansal and Abhijit Ogale, "Learning to Drive: Beyond Pure Imitation," *Waypoint* blog, Waymo, December 10, 2018.

[52] Shuyang Cheng, Yang Song, and Peisheng Li, "Using Automated Data Augmentation to Advance Our Waymo Driver," *Waypoint* blog, Waymo, April 2, 2020. This augmentation can include image rotation,

ing bad situations along with neural networks was, in 2019, producing positive experimental results. However, the 2019 blog post remained skeptical of DL for situations with limited training data. Recognizing the limitations of ML, Waymo trains its vehicles on the road using an approach that augments ML capabilities with "explicit reasoning" processes.[53]

Validation of the Waymo Driver system occurs through a series of testing, simulation, and operations on public roads.[54] Closed course testing occurs at Castle in Merced County, California, on a former Air Force base. On this closed course, Waymo can drive its vehicles throughout a lifelike community. The course contains roads of varying widths and shapes. Engineers can create obstacles and other situations that might occur in real life. For example, they can include cyclists or trucks dropping trash on the road.

The closed course testing draws on a large database of real-world data and the creativity of the engineers. The information gathered from both the real-world data and closed course tests are used to develop simulations. The combination of closed course testing and computer-based simulation contributes to training the Waymo Driver system. The use of both methods enables the Waymo team to individually assess the components within the system as needed. A fully integrated test that assesses the hardware and the software is accomplished with the closed course testing. Finally, the Waymo Driver system undergoes testing on public roads without riders and, eventually, with riders during the testing phase. The intent is for the Driver to continuously learn from all of these test, simulation, and operations phases.

Despite the data gathered and creatively imagined scenarios, challenges are still encountered. For example, a Waymo Driver (during a fully autonomous test with a rider on a public road) was challenged by the placement of traffic cones on the road.[55] The cones were not contained in the previously mapped dataset, so the vehicle was uncertain how to respond. The Driver stopped and appeared to be assessing the situation, then started moving again and then stopped. The vehicle was eventually driven in manual mode, but the failure served as a good opportunity for Waymo to train its Driver software on how to respond to traffic cones. Once the new training is completed, the updated Driver software will be shared with the fleet of Waymo vehicles.

---

color changes, and distortions; see Ekin Dogus Cubuk and Barret Zoph, "Improving Deep Learning Performance with AutoAugment," Google Research blog, June 4, 2018; Ekin D. Cubuk, Barret Zoph, Jonathon Shlens, and Quoc V. Le, "RandAugment: Practical Automated Data Augmentation with a Reduced Search Space," version 2, arXiv preprint arXiv:1909.13719, November 14, 2019.

[53] Waymo, "Scale AI's TransformX Presentation with Waymo Head of Research Drago Anguelov," video, October 20, 2021b.

[54] Waymo, "The Waymo Driver's Training Regimen: How Structured Testing Prepares Our Self-Driving Technology for the Real World," *Waypoint* blog, September 10, 2020.

[55] JJRicks Studios, "Waymo Self Driving Taxi Goes Rogue: Blocks Traffic, Evades Capture | JJRicks Rides with Waymo #54," video, undated.

Voyage

Voyage developed an open-source self-driving simulator called Deepdrive. The simulator is intended to provide an area for researchers to test and explore their agents without needing physical hardware.[56] Sensor data and maps are provided for use in a 3D simulation. Deep RL and IL provide the baseline agents for this Python-based software toolkit. The simulation enables people to develop agents and test the success of reward functions according to such parameters as speed and legality.[57]

GM Cruise

Voyage was a spin-off of Udacity and now has been acquired (as of 2021) by GM Cruise. Cruise uses ML to predict behavior: "The biggest challenge with prediction is not building a system that is able to handle the nominal cases well, but rather building something that generalizes well to uncommon situations and does so accurately."[58] The Cruise system tackles the challenge of rarity through upsampling: "we focus on finding the needle in the haystack of regular driving and use upsampling to teach the models more about these events."[59]

One approach is to develop a detector that specifically identifies long-tail events, such as U-turns or K-turns. This detector could collect data on the unique and specified situation of a U-turn event. However, the detector approach identifies discrete events and does not scale well for other unique long-tail situations. In other words, the approach of simply writing detectors for every imaginable long-tail situation is not scalable in a world of numerous potential events.

The Cruise system has a self-supervised learning framework that compares the predicted and observed trajectories. Consider the situation in which the system predicted a car turning left, but the car instead proceeded straight through the intersection. For this scenario, the prediction was incorrect, so the system automatically labels the prediction as such. Such a system reduces the need for manual identification. Any errors that occur, such as that described in the left-turn example, are marked as such. The system then upsamples data from these error events to ensure that the dataset is not biased toward those scenarios already solved. In this way, the dataset scales as needed for the long-tail events. This system has demonstrated success with long-tail events, such as U-turns, K-turns, and a variety of cut-ins by vehicles.

---

[56] Drew Gray, "Introducing Voyage Deepdrive," *Voyage*, November 13, 2019.

[57] "Voyage Launches Open-Source Self-Driving Simulation Platform," *Robotics Business Review*, November 14, 2019.

[58] Sean Harris, "Cruise's Continuous Learning Machine Predicts the Unpredictable on San Francisco Roads," *Cruise*, September 10, 2020.

[59] Harris, 2020.

Mobileye

Mobileye, an Israeli company, was acquired by Intel in 2017.[60] Mobileye has permits to test its autonomous systems in multiple countries and in 2021 received approval to test its vehicles in New York City.[61] One of its first products was a custom semiconductor chip designed for large computational loads to handle Mobileye's audiovisual systems, called EyeQ. Mobileye has a wide range of advanced driver assistance systems (ADASs), with different levels of automated actions depending on how passive or active the system is. These features are dependent on the type of ADAS used. A passive system includes forward collision warning (FCW), alerting the driver of a potential collision, while an active system can include Automatic Emergency Braking. These ADAS products have been sold to multiple companies, including Audi and BMW.[62] On December 6, 2021, Intel announced its intention of taking the company public.[63] In particular, Intel has seen success with the FCW system, with multiple studies reporting significant collision reduction. For example, Yoshida Taxi Company found collision reduction of up to 85 percent once its cars were fitted with the system.[64]

Mobileye's RL development lies in its driving policy, which predicts human driver behavior from other cars to execute a driving decision in response. The training preference is to greedily absorb training data to make incremental decisions. While Mobileye uses deep neural networks as a main model, the novel concept for its RL model is the idea of IL. Instead of building an objective function to optimize a set of behaviors, Mobileye's engineers simulate the objective function because of the complicated nature of building a function to predict human behavior. The idea is to train the vehicle system through increasingly complex simulations. One key piece the engineers note is that they do not use a Markov decision process in their model. They state that even though most RL models use this, they do not feel comfortable given how unpredictable human driving can be.[65]

The redundant system that Mobileye's engineers have in place for driving policy is a mathematical model that they developed called Responsibility-Sensitive Safety (RSS). The idea is to have a white box, interpretable model to ensure safety for autonomous driving. The model estimates reasonable safe driving behavior, formalizing an interpretation of "duty of care"

---

60 Andrew J. Hawkins, "Intel Is Taking Its Self-Driving Company Mobileye Public in 2022," *The Verge*, December 7, 2021b.

61 Andrew J. Hawkins, "Intel's Mobileye Begins Testing Autonomous Vehicles in New York City," *The Verge*, July 20, 2021a.

62 Mobileye, "Rethinking Technology for the Autonomous Future," webpage, undated-b.

63 Intel, "Intel Announces Intent to Take Mobileye Public," press release, December 6, 2021.

64 Mobileye, "Japan: Yoshida Taxi Company Lowers Collisions Rates by 85% with Mobileye Technology," webpage, undated-a.

65 Shai Shalev-Shwartz, Shaked Shammah, and Amnon Shashua, "Safe, Multi-Agent, Reinforcement Learning for Autonomous Driving," arXiv preprint arXiv:1610.03295, October 11, 2016.

from tort law.[66] The goal is to ensure that the autonomous system is never the cause of an accident, and thus a framework of equations is developed from these concepts. The equations are derived from basic mechanical equations. These equations are used for calculating safe distance between cars such that they are within safe braking distance. They include safe longitudinal and safe lateral distances. The RSS model is used for validating the main RL model and is used as a fail-safe against the RL model to reduce accidents that the autonomous vehicle could cause. If the distances pass some dangerous threshold in the RSS model, it overrides the RL prediction outputs.[67]

The following are observations from the field of autonomous driving:

1. Autonomous driving has advantages for generating training examples because driving is an activity in which drivers can lead the technology through many examples in the normal course of operation, including low-probability scenarios important to capture. For example, Waymo claims to have trained over 1 million miles of rider-only (taxi-like) operation in Arizona and California with just 20 vehicle contacts; none of the contacts reported injuries.[68] Overall, Waymo boasts on its homepage, "Over 20 billion real world and simulated miles driven."[69] Any DoD application would likely need similar access to real-world examples, which might be limiting in terms of the application space available to DoD.
2. Cases that occurred infrequently can be difficult to capture and train against. Such cases are especially problematic when an adversary might be intentionally attempting to undermine the system, as has been the case in such systems.[70] A simple adversarial example is to intentionally project lines on the road to cause the vehicle to swerve into oncoming traffic.[71] A DoD application would likely face active adversaries attempting to undermine an RL system. Any method to harden a system against adversarial

[66] *Duty of care* is defined as the "obligation to avoid negligence, particularly to take reasonable care not to cause physical, economic, or emotional loss or harm to others" ("Duty of Care," *Oxford Reference* entry, Oxford University Press, undated).

[67] Shai Shalev-Shwartz, Shaked Shammah, and Amnon Shashua, "On a Formal Model of Safe and Scalable Self-Driving Cars," Mobileye, 2017.

[68] Trent Victor, Kristofer Kusano, Tilia Gode, Ruoshu Chen, and Matthew Schwall, *Safety Performance of the Waymo Rider-Only Automated Driving System at One Million Miles*, Waymo, 2023.

[69] Waymo, homepage, undated.

[70] Ambra Demontis, Maura Pintor, Luca Demetrio, Kathrin Grosse, Hsiao-Ying Lin, Chengfang Fang, Battista Biggio, and Fabio Roli, "A Survey on Reinforcement Learning Security with Application to Autonomous Driving," arXiv preprint arXiv:2212.06123, 2022.

[71] A. Boloor, X. He, C. Gill, Y. Vorobeychik, and X. Zhang, "Simple Physical Adversarial Examples Against End-to-End Autonomous Driving Models," *Proceedings of the 2019 IEEE International Conference on Embedded Software and Systems (ICESS)*, 2019; Pengfei Jing, Qiyi Tang, Yuefeng Du, Lei Xue, Xiapu Luo, Ting Wang, Sen Nie, and Shi Wu, "Too Good to Be Safe: Tricking Lane Detection in Autonomous Driving with Crafted Perturbations," *Proceedings of USENIX Security Symposium*, 2021.

attacks would have to be generalized across the domains of the application, a requirement that may be difficult in complex applications.[72] The risk in this case is that an active adversary might find a weakness that can be exploited in operation with little time to retrain, test, and deploy the system updates to counter such attack and its variations.

3. RL development is costly. A careful analysis of alternatives should be made in advance to determine the total cost and benefit of any RL-based application. As an example, it is estimated that Google spent over $1.1 billion on autonomous driving from 2009 to the end of 2015,[73] with an estimate of $3.5 billion for research and development by 2020.[74]
4. RL is often a task in a process to solve rather than a general approach to a large-scale problem. Other processes, not always AI-based, often supplement RL, as in the Waymo approach in which ML was augmented with "explicit reasoning."[75]

Application Suitability of RL for Broad DoD Problems

As discussed in Chapter 1, RL has been very successful in learning and winning at games with varying degrees of complexity. Transitioning to real-world applications results in challenges related to problem complexity, size, and the difficulty that RL has in learning from limited training data with subsequent generalization across domain shifts. The examples of autonomous driving showed that, even with a problem in which many driving examples can be collected, the systems can still struggle with unanticipated shifts in the environment, such as a shadow cast in the road. A recent survey of autonomous driving further discussed challenges to overcome in this type of application, with the following conclusion:

> Overall, many problems in this area remain to be addressed, such as environmental detail and sensor simulation, computational specifications, transferability to actual systems, robustness, and agent validation. Due to these concerns, it can be claimed that reinforcement learning is not an adequate method for automotive motion planning. However, when combined with other approaches, it can be very useful in solving complex optimization challenges.[76]

---

[72] Y. Liu, C. Wu, X. Xi, Y. Li, G. Cao, W. Cao, and H. Wang, "Adversarial Discriminative Feature Separation for Generalization in Reinforcement Learning," *Proceedings of the 2022 International Joint Conference on Neural Networks (IJCNN)*, 2022.

[73] Mark Harris, "Google Has Spent over $1.1 Billion on Self-Driving Tech," *IEEE Spectrum*, September 15, 2017.

[74] Robert Baldwin, "Self-Driving-Car Research Has Cost $16 Billion. What Do We Have to Show for It?" *Car and Driver*, February 10, 2020.

[75] Waymo, 2021b.

[76] B. Udugama, "Review of Deep Reinforcement Learning for Autonomous Driving," arXiv preprint arXiv:2302.06370, 2023.

Such an assessment notwithstanding, the financial incentive to success and the resources being sunk into autonomous driving have already resulted in partially autonomous, or *driver-assisted*, vehicles.[77] Given the rapid progress in AI, it is likely that autonomous driving may become an example of a complex, real-world application in which RL plays a role. Its relevance to DoD could lie in similar applications of complex motion planning, such as logistics movement or real-time route planning and control.

As shown in Figure 1.1, autonomous driving may be classified as mostly a "narrow" problem with complexities in the environment and challenges to robustness in the environment. Where within the "narrow to broad" application space would we expect RL to be a feasible approach for DoD to consider, at least with a near-term (five- to ten-year) perspective? Such a question is, in part, a moving target as computational power advances, RL algorithms advance, and more real-world examples are developed.

Li discusses various applications in which RL is used in production systems—i.e., deployed systems rather than subjects of academic papers.[78] These include systems from Google for content recommendation[79] and computer chip layout;[80] systems from Microsoft to make contextual decisions[81] and tools to support automation systems;[82] and, from Didi, a ride-sharing dispatch application.[83] These, as well as other applications listed as promising in academic studies,[84] have elements that may indicate where RL is suited:

1. applications in which the domains are well characterized (e.g., gaming) and in which large training datasets are available (e.g., content recommendation) or are conducive to simulation (e.g., control theory, gaming)

---

[77] Cherise Threewitt, "10 Vehicles That Are Almost Self-Driving in 2023," *U.S. News and World Report*, April 20, 2023.

[78] Yuxi Li, "Reinforcement Learning in Practice: Opportunities and Challenges," arXiv preprint arXiv:2202.11296, 2022.

[79] Minmin Chen, Alex Beutel, Paul Covington, Sagar Jain, Francois Belletti, and Ed H. Chi, "Top-K Off-Policy Correction for a REINFORCE Recommender System," *Proceedings of the Twelfth ACM International Conference on Web Search and Data Mining*, 2019.

[80] Azalia Mirhoseini, Anna Goldie, Mustafa Yazgan, Joe Wenjie Jiang, Ebrahim Songhori, Shen Wang, Young-Joon Lee, Eric Johnson, Omkar Pathak, and Azade Nazi, "A Graph Placement Methodology for Fast Chip Design," *Nature*, Vol. 594, No. 7862, 2021.

[81] Alekh Agarwal, Sarah Bird, Markus Cozowicz, Luong Hoang, John Langford, Stephen Lee, Jiaji Li, Dan Melamed, Gal Oshri, and Oswaldo Ribas, "Making Contextual Decisions with Low Technical Debt," arXiv preprint arXiv:1606.03966, 2016.

[82] Microsoft, "Build AI Without Data Science," webpage, undated.

[83] Zhiwei Qin, Xiaocheng Tang, Yan Jiao, Fan Zhang, Zhe Xu, Hongtu Zhu, and Jieping Ye, "Ride-Hailing Order Dispatching at Didi via Reinforcement Learning," *INFORMS Journal on Applied Analytics*, Vol. 50, No. 5, 2020.

[84] Li, 2022.

2. optimization applications (e.g., computer chip layout, route planning) or applications with clearly defined and expressible goals (e.g., automation tasks, robotics)
3. applications that can show clear competitive advantage over existing technology (automated versus manual ride sharing dispatch).

Most of the applications fall within the narrow AI category of Figure 1.1, with some crossover into the broader AI category. This list is not intended to be definitive or exhaustive, however, especially given how few real-world applications of RL are reported. Some applications use RL as part of a larger system, such as ChatGPT, which used RL to fine-tune the behavior of GPT-3.5.[85] Since algorithms are often carefully crafted for particular applications, businesses likely consider implementation details proprietary.

Table 2.4 summarizes from the reviewed literature observed and expected risks for narrow problems (approaching the level of complex games), autonomous driving (narrow in the sense of a task to perform but complex in its overall environment), and broad DoD problems (complex in many domains). By default, risks are expected to be *medium* in narrow applications and *high* in broad applications when identified as vulnerabilities in the literature. In the autonomous driving application, considerable development has reduced some of risks

TABLE 2.4

Summary of Observed or Expected RL Risks for Three Types of Problems

Category of Risk	Description	Narrow Problems	Autonomous Driving	DoD Broad Problems	Takeaway
Unrealistic expectations	Misunderstanding of AI capabilities	Medium	Low	High	RL capabilities do not necessarily follow intuitive leaps of ability ascribed by humans.
	Thinking too big	Medium	Medium	High	Risk areas tend to grow with problem size using RL, and addressing all may become difficult.
Use case–related issues	Missing value or cost-benefit ratio	Medium	Low	High	Is RL the best approach?
	Complexity	Medium	High	High	Problem complexity can easily outpace computational capabilities and data demands.
Organizational constraints	Cost	Medium	High	High	Large applications are currently the domain of big technology firms with high sunk costs.

85 Sandra Mitrović, Davide Andreoletti, and Omran Ayoub, "ChatGPT or Human? Detect and Explain. Explaining Decisions of Machine Learning Model for Detecting Short ChatGPT-Generated Text," arXiv preprint arXiv:2301.13852, 2023.

Table 2.4—Continued

Category of Risk	Description	Narrow Problems	Autonomous Driving	DoD Broad Problems	Takeaway
Lack of key resources	Lack of employees with expertise	Medium	Low	High	RL algorithms finely tuned by deep specialists are in short supply.
	Data availability	Medium	Low	High	Real-world applications require large sets of real-world data to train against.
Technological	Identifying the need to retrain	Medium	Medium	High	Long, complex sequences in broad problems make poor outcomes harder to identify.
	Retraining feasibility	Medium	Medium	High	The need to retrain often comes from low-probability outlier events that are difficult find and train RL against.
	Too difficult to model or diverges from reality	Medium	Medium	High	It is often difficult to model broad problems and capture all relevant cases needed to effectively train RL.
	Lack of explainability/ trust	Medium	Low	High	Broad problems may have too many cases against which to test RL and develop trust.
	Safe operation	Medium	Medium	High	Safe operation is easier to define given the smaller domain of narrow problems.
	Incomplete model/response to uncertainty	Medium	High	High	Uncertainties in broad problems may be too numerous to model or simply unknown in nature.
	Reward hacking	Medium	Medium	High	As problems become broader, how to define a reward function becomes more difficult.
	Adversarial attack	Medium	High	High	Even narrow RL is subject to adversarial attacks, but broader problems have greater potential for many more.

NOTE: *Low*, *medium*, and *high* refer to the level of risk for use of RL.

(shown as *low*), whereas others might be found to have been greater than expected (shown as *high*). While not rigorous, the table illustrates the multidimensional nature of factors needed in considering risk. The technical risks in this table will be used within the guided workshop discussed in Chapter 4 for evaluation within a broad DoD application.

Conclusions

RL is a technology that can provide strong advantages in the complex but simulated environments of gaming, as discussed in Chapter 1. As RL systems are scaled in size and transitioned to real world systems, however, both training requirements and the potential for failure mechanisms scale as well. As RL models become more complex, training from simulation may be limiting in terms of data generation, data latency, and even electrical power requirements. Further, training with real world data is needed to ensure that systems operate properly in realistic scenarios. The ability to train repeatedly in the real world, along with training around low-probability, high-consequence events, likely limits the application space for DoD that is suited for RL. The commercial example of autonomous driving illustrates the development and training costs needed to bring viable systems to market. Scaling RL systems to broader, more complex problems will likely need further advancements in algorithms beyond what is provided by scaling the amount of training data and DNN complexity, as these scale at a faster rate than Moore's law advancements in computational power.

CHAPTER 3

Scenarios for Exploring Challenges

This chapter describes a pair of scenarios that were developed by the project team to help provide context for the exploration of challenges that could arise from the fielding and operational use of RL systems for DoD applications. We begin by briefly discussing the selected DoD application domain that is common to both scenarios. We then describe a pair of hypothetical alternate pathways involving the fielding and employment of RL systems, which we refer to as *deployment scenarios*. The first deployment scenario features a more gradual, stepwise approach to achieve a desired end state. The second deployment scenario envisions a more ambitious "moon shot" approach, which seeks to achieve the desired end state in one fell swoop.

The Application Domain

In consultation with the sponsor, we selected operational-level command and control (C2) as the DoD application domain to serve as the focus area for the study. The air operations center (AOC) is a prime example of this type of capability, enabling a joint force air component commander (JFACC) to orchestrate the application of airpower in pursuit of joint force objectives. AOCs typically operate according to the air tasking cycle (ATC), depicted in Figure 3.1.

The six-phase ATC represents a nominal 72-hour process. One of the key outputs of this process is the air tasking order (ATO), which nominally covers a 24-hour period of air operations. Thus, while some elements of an AOC may be involved in overseeing the execution of the current day's ATO, other elements of the AOC are busy planning for the next two days' worth of ATOs.[1] This lengthy planning process and reported process and staffing biases favoring deliberate over dynamic targeting will naturally draw the attention of those seeking to apply RL (and AI more generally)[2] to improve the speed and flexibility of operational-level C2 entities, such as the AOC. This draw magnifies the importance of gaining an understand-

---

1 Sherrill Lingel, Jeff Hagen, Eric Hastings, Mary Lee, Matthew Sargent, Matthew Walsh, Li Ang Zhang, and David Blancett, *Joint All-Domain Command and Control for Modern Warfare: An Analytic Framework for Identifying and Developing Artificial Intelligence Applications*, RAND Corporation, RR-A4408/1-AF, 2020.

2 Lingel et al., 2020.

FIGURE 3.1
Air Tasking Cycle

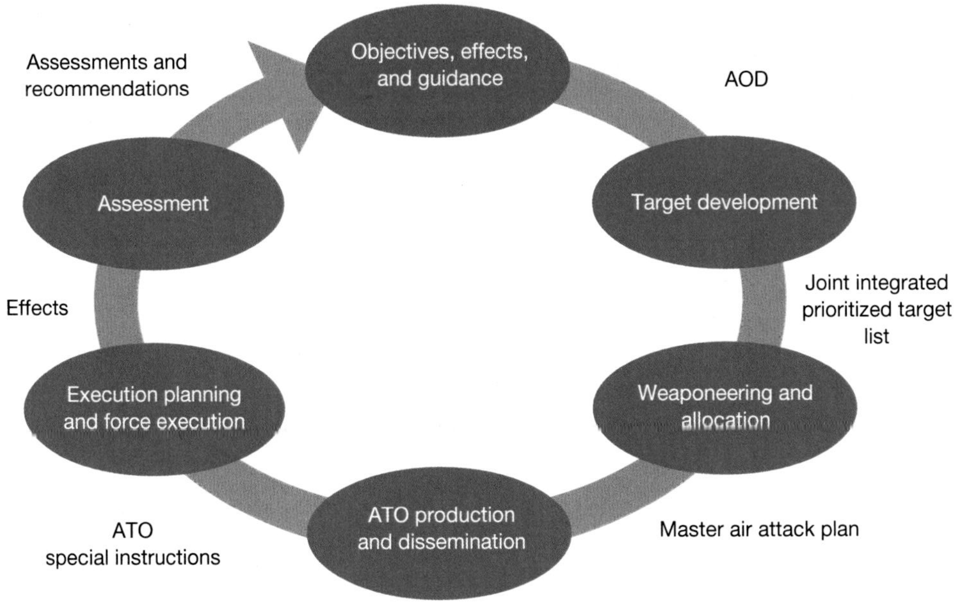

SOURCE: Adapted from Lingel et al., 2020.

ing of the potential challenges involved with deploying RL systems for operational-level C2 applications. Moreover, given the high degree of similarity between the ATC and the joint targeting cycle, insights on challenges involved with deploying RL systems to support the ATC and/or the AOC could potentially apply to the processes of other operational-level C2 entities as well, such as a future multidomain task force or theater fires command.[3]

Crawl-Walk-Run Scenario

Inspired by a string of notable successes in applying RL to games, researchers seek to apply RL to a wide range of DoD problems, including enhancing operational-level C2 processes. Most prominent among these efforts are projects aiming to accelerate the nominal 72-hour ATC within the AOC and improve its capability and capacity to conduct dynamic targeting. Eventually, several RL-based solutions demonstrate the potential of AI-accelerated C2 capa-

[3] See Kyle David Borne, "Targeting in Multi-Domain Operations," *Military Review*, Vol. 99, 2019.

bilities and succeed in crossing the technology development "valley of death" and are fielded.[4] An overview of the scenario is depicted in Figure 3.2.

Initially, for the "crawl" stage, the RL agents or systems are deployed on a limited, small-scale basis within the AOC (left side of Figure 3.2). These systems are employed for fairly narrow applications where other more-traditional methods are too slow—such as supporting dynamic targeting with rapid route planning and replanning for intelligence, surveillance, and reconnaissance assets to find, fix, and track targets of opportunity or to augment existing mission planning tools. Staffing levels within the AOC fluctuate slightly as the new systems are absorbed, but, overall, the number of personnel remains largely status quo.

As the technological state of the art advances, the AOC transitions over time from the "crawl" stage to the "walk" stage (middle of Figure 3.2). Greater numbers of RL agents or systems are deployed more extensively throughout the AOC, teamed with human supervisors. Some of these RL agents continue to serve in relatively narrow applications, but others begin to take over greater ranges of functions, leading to the retirement of several legacy planning tools. Eventually, encouraged by early positive operational experiences with the AI-accelerated, more dynamic AOC, commanders begin to reduce staffing levels, reassigning personnel to help fill other high-priority demands for military personnel. At the conclusion

FIGURE 3.2
Scenario Overview—Crawl-Walk-Run

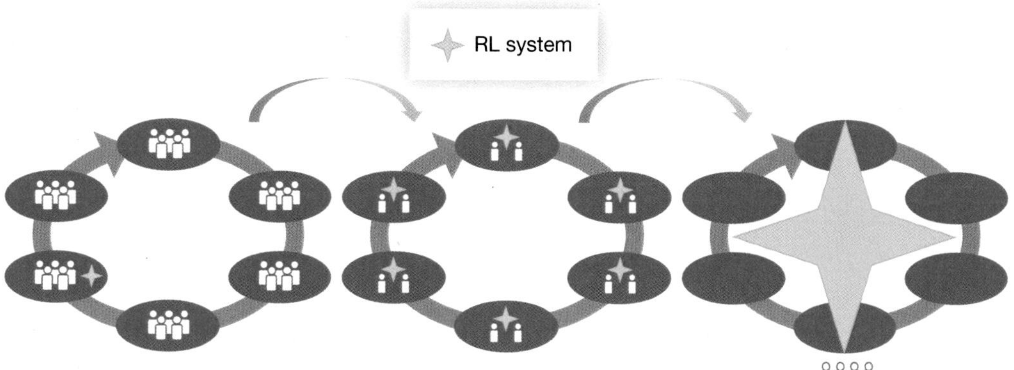

- Limited, small-scale deployments of RL agents/systems
- Staffing levels largely status quo

- Multiple RL agents/systems teamed with human supervisors
- Staffing levels reduced but allow for 24/7 human supervision oversight

- Single, large RL agent/system operating nearly autonomously
- Minimal staffing to ensure care and feeding of RL system, comms are online, etc.

NOTE: Comms = communications.

---

[4] *Valley of death* refers to the period from initial technology development through to operational capabilities, in which sustained funding is most difficult to obtain.

of the rightsizing efforts, the reduced staffing levels are sufficient to allow for 24/7 human supervision of the RL systems but are significantly below staffing levels associated with a "traditional" AOC.

Continued advances in technology, combined with pressure to win the AI arms race with China, leads to the "run" stage—the deployment of a single, large-scale RL system capable of fulfilling all the functions of an AOC nearly autonomously (right side of Figure 3.2). Humans are largely out of the loop, although there are override features built into the system that can be triggered under in extreme circumstances. AOC staffing is reduced to the bare minimum necessary to provide for the "care and feeding" of the RL system and to ensure that the required enablers, such as communications networks, are functioning within acceptable bounds.

The Great Leap Scenario

As with the crawl-walk-run scenario, researchers inspired by a string of notable successes in applying RL to games seek to apply RL to a wide range of DoD problems, including accelerating the nominal 72-hour ATC within the AOC and improving its capability and capacity to conduct dynamic targeting. Eventually, several RL-based solutions demonstrate the potential of AI-accelerated C2 capabilities and succeed in crossing the technology development "valley of death" and are fielded. In parallel, the continuing research drive to advance the state of the art in AI in general and RL in particular achieves a series of key breakthroughs, making the

FIGURE 3.3
Scenario Overview—the Great Leap

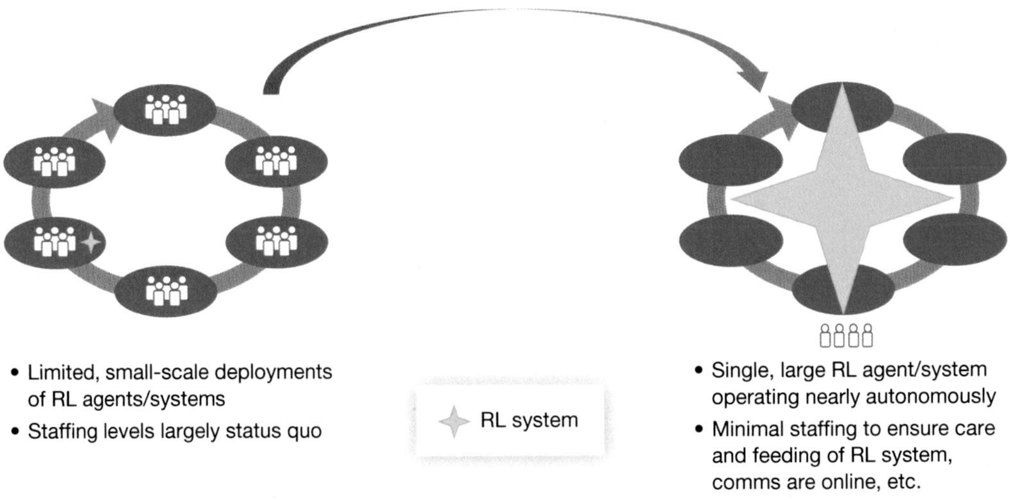

NOTE: Comms = communications.

prospects of a broader solution to operational-level C2 problems seemingly within reach. An overview of this scenario is depicted in Figure 3.3.

The starting point for this deployment scenario is basically identical to the that of the "crawl" stage of the crawl-walk-run scenario. Initially, the RL agents or systems are deployed on a limited, small-scale basis within the AOC (left side of Figure 3.3). These systems are employed for rather narrow applications for which other more-traditional methods are too slow. Staffing levels within the AOC fluctuate slightly but, overall, remain largely status quo.

Pressure to win the AI arms race with China combined with rapid advances in AI and RL technology lead DoD researchers and AI developers to pursue a "moon shot" effort to field a single, large-scale RL system capable of fulfilling all the functions of an AOC nearly autonomously (right side of Figure 3.3). Ultimately, these efforts yield a system capable of performing all the required functions of an AOC much more rapidly and flexibly than a "traditional" AOC. Humans are largely out of the loop, although there are override features built into the system that can be triggered under extreme circumstances. AOC staffing is reduced to the bare minimum necessary to maintain the RL system and to ensure that the required enablers, such as communications networks, are functioning within acceptable bounds.

During the structured elicitation workshop discussed in Chapter 4, the great leap scenario was referred to as the "gonculator" approach,[5] in the sense that the resulting RL technology would consist of a large, complex system into which all available data collected from the ATC of Figure 3.1 is fed to receive a resulting decision output.

---

5 The *gonculator*, in Air Force usage, represents "a mythical, mysterious problem-solving machine that crunches overwhelming masses of data and then offers an optimal solution." See Angelle Khachadoorian, Air Force Culture and Language Center, Maxwell Air Force Base, "Speaking Air Forcefully: The Gonculator Knows Best," March 18, 2022.

CHAPTER 4

Challenge Identification Framework and Workshop

We employed a structured elicitation approach to identify the key issues from the interaction between RL technologies and DoD. We wanted to draw out the challenges that could be associated with developing RL systems for a complex military scenario and identify potential force restructuring and technical challenges associated with employing RL in a DoD application, along with their implications and potential mitigation strategies.

The Structured Elicitation Framework

We adapted a structured elicitation method from prior work that has been conducted in this field.[1] Using this, we developed a mixed-method approach, gathering input over three sessions of an all-day workshop with RAND and DoD personnel (see Appendix A for more information). The first session focused on force restructuring challenges, the second session was on technical challenges, and the third session was used to evaluate the challenges based on several evaluation statements.

At the beginning of each session, we briefed a complex military scenario to which RL could be applied in the future. Each session was broken into two subsections: Crawl-Walk-Run and Great Leap for the force restructuring session and Walk and Run for the technical challenges session. After the briefing, we asked participants to spend time individually identifying, and then discussing as a group, concerns that they identified as being associated with either force restructuring or technical challenges. We provided the challenges (see Table 2.3) in the session on technical challenges because our participants were not all experts in AI or RL, and we felt it was more important for the participants to focus on the implications and possible mitigations associated with each.

In the third session, we asked participants to rank challenges according to what they think should be the top priority for DoD. Prioritization was ranked from 1 to *N* within each subsec-

[1] See Lauren A. Mayer, Jon Schmid, Sydney Litterer, and Marjory S. Blumenthal, *A Structured Elicitation Approach to Identify Technology-Based Challenges: With Application to Inform Force Planning for Technological Surprise*, RAND Corporation, RR-A701-1, 2021, p. ix.

tion. For instance, challenges within the force restructuring and Crawl-Walk-Run subsection were ranked from 1 to 14 because 14 challenges were identified, whereas the Great Leap subsection was ranked only from 1 to 8. We then developed a closed-ended survey to evaluate the challenges based on six criteria related to the severity of the challenge, likelihood, and other factors for each scenario considered (Table 4.1 and Chapter 3).

At the end of the workshop, time was devoted to discussing additional issues that might have come from a larger perspective gained from the previous sessions. It was also an opportunity for participants to summarize their thoughts on issues discussed.

Results

At the close of the workshop, we collected all completed closed-ended survey evaluations. Because the RAND team and the sponsor were not asked to complete evaluation surveys, there were ten completed surveys for this analysis. The mean score for each challenge is shown in Table 4.2. This table shows the top three challenges for each subsection according to participant ranking in the priority category. Numbers in the remaining columns depict the mean score for each evaluation statement taken across all participants, and p-values at or greater than the 95-percent, 98-percent, and 99-percent confidence intervals are noted.[2]

TABLE 4.1
The Categories and Descriptions for Rating Challenges

Category of Effect	Description
Barriers to DoD detection and prevention	DoD is unlikely to detect this challenge prior to its being realized or to prevent it from being realized even if it is detected (e.g., because of a lack of ability or willingness, or other barriers).
Other barriers	Other than barriers to DoD detection and prevention, there are very few barriers that could keep this challenge from being realized (barriers may include, e.g., lack of technology readiness or adversary ability or intent to adopt technology, forces that change external factors, U.S. institutional or cultural incentives).
Mitigation difficulty	If this challenge is realized, it will be difficult for DoD to mitigate its impact (e.g., through authorities, capability, knowledge, costs, effort, time).
Impact on operations	Left unmitigated, this challenge will severely limit (directly or indirectly) DoD's options for performing operations.
Impact on national security	Left unmitigated, this challenge will severely compromise (directly or indirectly) U.S. national security (e.g., via changes to economy, culture, politics, military operations).
Likelihood of occurrence	This challenge is likely to occur given the scenario presented.

2 A p-value is a measure of the probability that the observed outcome is due to chance. See, for example, Ryan Winters, Andrew Winters, and Ronald G. Amedee, "Statistics: A Brief Overview," *Ochsner Journal*, Vol. 10, No. 3, 2010.

TABLE 4.2
Top Three Challenges, by Priority, by Workshop Subsection

		Challenge Description	Priority	Barriers to DoD Detection and Prevention	Other Barriers	Mitigation Difficulty	Impact on Operations	Impact on National Security	Likelihood of Occurrence
Force Restructuring	Crawl-Walk-Run	Department of the Air Force (DAF) and DoD lack workforce to deploy models, such as an ML career field, data cleaning skills	1	2.9	2.3	3.7	3.67	3.4	4.4[c]
		Recruitment and retention of a highly specialized workforce is hampered by higher pay outside DoD	2	3.9[b]	3.2	3.8[a]	3.5	3.3	3.8
		Operators lack training for supervisory control of RL agents and system	3	3.5	2.6	3.2	3.9[c]	3.4	3.9[c]
	Great Leap	No failure mode that is not catastrophic mission failure	1	3.9	3.1	4.1[b]	4.6[c]	4.7[c]	3.3
		Lack of trust and understanding of the system	2	3.3	2.5	3.6[b]	3.4	3.3	3.5
		Blind trust in the system	3	2.56	2.11	2.78	3.11	3.67	1.78

Force Restructuring

Participants identified a total of 22 challenges during the session on force restructuring (Table 4.3). A summary of all the challenges, their implications, and potential mitigations discussed during this session is available in Table B.1 in the appendix. In this section, we focus on the top three to five challenges according to participant prioritization for each deployment scenario (summarized in Table 4.2), their implications, and potential mitigations.[3] We then compare the potential impacts and consequences of the alternative pathways for deploying RL systems represented by the Crawl-Walk-Run and Great Leap scenarios.

[3] Participants identified a total of 14 challenges for the Crawl-Walk-Run scenario and eight distinct challenges for the Great Leap scenario. We focus on the top five and top three priority challenges for Crawl-Walk-Run and Great Leap, respectively, in this section, because they represent a similar proportion of each scenario's total.

Table 4.2—Continued

		Challenge Description	Priority	Barriers to DoD Detection and Prevention	Other Barriers	Mitigation Difficulty	Impact on Operations	Impact on National Security	Likelihood of Occurrence
Technical	Walk	Safe operation (RL can have side effect when pursuing rewards)	1	3.7[a]	3.1	3.5	3.78[b]	3.89[c]	3.5
		Identifying need for retraining; may not be able to identify in time	2	3.5	2.9	3.8[c]	3.6[b]	3.4	3.8[a]
		Incomplete model or response to uncertainty	3	3.33	3	3.33	3.55	3.44	3.56
	Run	Too difficult to model or dramatic model divergence from reality	1	3.4	3.5	4.1[c]	3.5	3.5	3.8
		Safe operation (RL can have side effect when pursuing rewards)	2	3.78[a]	2.56	3.44	3.78[b]	3.89[c]	3.56
		Identifying need for retraining	3	3.2	2.6	3.4	3.5	3.4	3.6

SOURCE: Author analysis of survey results.

NOTE: Evaluation statements were scored on a scale from strongly disagree (1) to strongly agree (5). Numbers shown represent the mean taken from ten completed participant surveys.

[a] *p*-value at or above the 95-percent confidence interval.

[b] *p*-value at or above the 98-percent confidence interval.

[c] *p*-value at or above the 99-percent confidence interval.

Crawl-Walk-Run

The top challenge identified and prioritized by our participants was that DAF and DoD more broadly lack a workforce with the requisite skills, knowledge, and expertise to deploy and sustain RL models and systems, such as an ML career field. This could engender a lack of understanding of what can and cannot be done with RL systems within DoD. This could also drive DoD to rely on an outside agency for the required expertise, perhaps even a nongovernment entity. Participants strongly agreed that this challenge would be likely to occur (mean score of 4.4). Participants also agreed that, left unmitigated, it could have a significant impact on operations and would be difficult for DoD to mitigate (both with mean scores of ~3.7).

Potential mitigation measures discussed included fostering the development of the required skills and expertise in the civilian workforce or an expanded engineering series, though that could pose other challenges as well without spare capacity. Outsourcing was also discussed as an option, but it was noted that that could bring other risks. Other options included relying on a federally funded research and development center (FFRDC) and putting ML practitioners into warrant officer positions (along with cyber practitioners). It was

TABLE 4.3
Top Force Restructuring Challenges

	Challenge Description	Priority	Barriers to DoD Detection and Prevention	Other Barriers	Mitigation Difficulty	Impact on Operations	Impact on National Security	Likelihood of Occurrence
Crawl-Walk-Run	DAF and DoD lack workforce to deploy models, such as an ML career field, data cleaning skills	1	2.9	2.3	3.7	3.67	3.4	4.4[c]
	Recruitment and retention of a highly specialized workforce is hampered by higher pay outside DoD	2	3.9[b]	3.2	3.8[a]	3.5	3.3	3.8
	Operators lack training for supervisory control of RL agents and system	3	3.5	2.6	3.2	3.9[c]	3.4	3.9[c]
	Staffing—overbooked, overtasked personnel	4	3.67	2.3	3.3	3.9[c]	3.2	4.1[c]
	Atrophy of battle planning workforce skill	5	3.2	2.5	3.5	3.7[c]	3.7[c]	3.4
Great Leap	No failure mode that is not catastrophic mission failure	1	3.9	3.1	4.1[b]	4.6[c]	4.7[c]	3.3
	Lack of trust and understanding of the system	2	3.3	2.5	3.6[b]	3.4	3.3	3.5
	Blind trust in the system	3	2.56	2.11	2.78	3.11	3.67	1.78

SOURCE: Author analysis of survey results.

NOTE: Evaluation statements were scored on a scale from strongly disagree (1) to strongly agree (5). Numbers shown represent the mean taken from ten completed participant surveys.

[a] *p*-value at or above the 95-percent confidence interval.

[b] *p*-value at or above the 98-percent confidence interval.

[c] *p*-value at or above the 99-percent confidence interval.

noted that the Army had tried this, but ML and cyber were challenging positions to fill and keep filled because the trained personnel could earn substantially more money elsewhere.

The challenge ranked as the second highest priority by participants sounded a similar note, centering on DoD's ability to recruit and retain a highly specialized workforce with the needed AI skill sets. Again, it was noted that these personnel would be able to make substantially greater sums of money outside the military. The result could be an insufficient workforce to employ and sustain RL systems. Participants discussed whether a system modeled on pilot retention bonuses could be effective in this case. This option has implications for the cost of the force, not just its composition. Participants agreed that this challenge would be difficult for DoD to avert (barriers to DoD detection and prevention score of 3.9) and mitigate (mitigation difficulty score of 3.8).

Potential mitigation options could include such measures as special incentive pay (although participants noted that it does not seem feasible to achieve parity with civilian salaries) and active-duty service commitments in exchange for training (and perhaps depending on the type of training and skills involved). Offering both training and immediate real-world opportunities, as well as possibly modifying enlistment standards for personnel in these positions, were also suggested as ways of enhancing DoD's ability to attract people with the needed skills.

The third-highest-priority challenge among participants was the lack of operator training for supervisory control of RL agents and systems. A central premise of the "walk" stage is that there are personnel with the necessary expertise to decide whether to accept the recommendation of an RL agent or system or to reject it and ask it to try again or shift to an alternate tool. Without this training, the human-agent teaming envisioned in the walk stage is not likely to function effectively. Participants strongly agreed that the challenge was likely to occur in this scenario and have a significant impact on operations (mean scores of 3.9). These operators need to be trained on the RL system sufficiently to understand where it works and where it does not. Such training is likely to be ongoing as systems are updated.

Overburdened or overtasked personnel was the fourth highest ranking priority challenge. Burdening overtasked personnel with yet another thing to do would likely result in the RL system not receiving the testing it deserves. If personnel are assigned additional tasks associated with RL systems without lowering or mitigating other existing demands, the system will not get the care and feeding required to confirm that it will work. Participants strongly agreed that this challenge was likely to occur (mean score of 4.1) and would have a significant impact on operations (mean score of 3.9). This challenge could be mitigated by expanding the workforce commensurate with the additional demands related to testing or employing the RL system.

Finally, the atrophying of battle planning workforce skills was the next highest ranking priority challenge. The introduction of RL systems could result in fewer opportunities for the workforce to exercise its battle planning skills, leading to a loss of proficiency over time. If the RL system fails or needs to be taken offline, the workforce may not be able to effectively plan and oversee operations. Participants strongly agreed that this challenge would have a significant impact on operations and national security (mean scores of 3.7). Continuing to train human planners and employing adaptive automation were identified as potential mitigations.

Great Leap

The highest-priority challenge for the Great Leap scenario was the observation that there was no failure mode that would not lead to catastrophic mission failure. Participants strongly agreed that this challenge would have a significant impact on operations and national security (mean scores of 4.3 and 4.4, respectively). They also strongly agreed that it would be difficult to mitigate (mean score of 4.1). A potential mitigation would be to establish a geographically separate backup AOC (perhaps in the continental United States) that is not being run by RL. Both AOCs could be employed during exercises, and the two AOCs could be cross-checked afterward, which could help build trust that the RL AOC is functioning properly.

The second and third highest priority challenges both deal with trust—a lack of trust and understanding of the systems on the one hand and blind trust in the system on the other. Both are problematic. Some operators could be highly skeptical and basically never trust the system. Others, perhaps following an earlier period of skepticism, could just accept any recommendation made by the RL system on blind faith. Participants agreed that overcoming a lack of trust could be a difficult proposition (mean score for mitigation difficulty of 3.6). Participants also seemed to agree that blind trust could have a significant impact on national security (mean score of ~3.7).

Crawl-Walk-Run Versus Great Leap

Among all force restructuring challenges, "no failure mode that is not catastrophic mission failure," the highest priority challenge in the Great Leap scenario, stands out. Participants strongly agreed that this challenge would have severe impacts on both operations (4.6) and national security (4.7). Moreover, participants agreed (4.1) that this challenge would be very difficult to mitigate.

From Figures 4.1 and 4.2, we can conclude that perceptions of the Great Leap to spring AI forward in one swoop are that this approach would have a higher impact on both operations and national security compared with the Crawl-Walk-Run approach.[4] While the majority of the data are clustered in a high likelihood of occurring but not as damaging, three distinct challenges associated with the Great Leap are perceived to have a much higher impact on national security than the others (Table 4.4):

1. Great Leap (GL)1: no failure mode that is not catastrophic mission failure
2. GL4: less oversight involved and visibility (observability) into when the RL errs is exacerbated by Great Leap approach
3. GL7: turning it over to killer robots or RL systems.

We can see that the average of the perception for the highest priority challenge in the Great Leap scenario (GL1) could heavily affect national security and is close to at least half the

[4] We focus on the discussion of these two criteria because many of the challenges were scored by participants with a 99-percent confidence interval along these dimensions, as shown in Table 4.2.

FIGURE 4.1
Force Restructuring—Average Impact on National Security Versus Average Likelihood

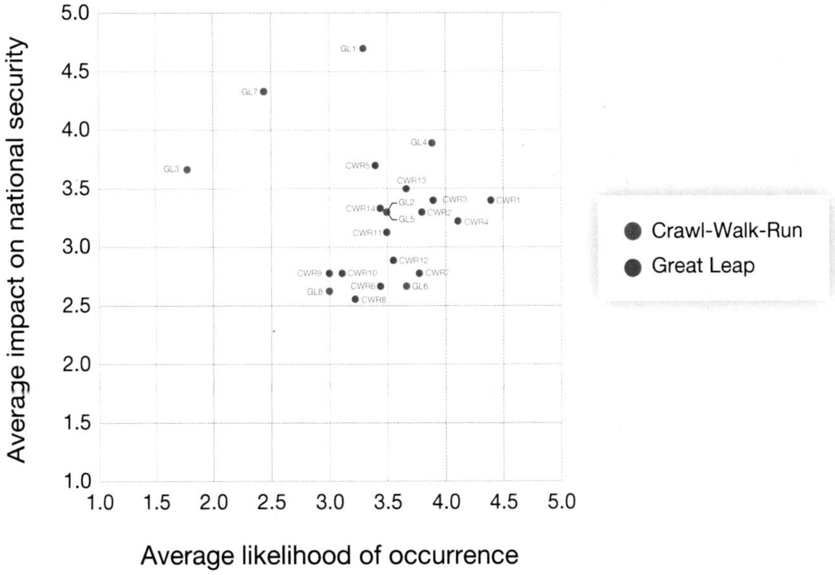

SOURCE: Author analysis of survey results.
NOTE: See Table 4.4 for corresponding graph codes.

challenges regarding likelihood. The high priority for this challenge, along with its perceived high impact, suggests that experts are concerned about doing a rapid shift into AI with complete replacements (i.e., Great Leap). Conversely, the Crawl-Walk-Run challenges appeared to be less concerning to participants, as the challenges center on a score of 3.5 for likelihood and 3.0 for impact on national security. This suggests that adopting a Great Leap approach could be too risky to be a feasible course of action. Figure 4.2, depicting data on the impact on operations, similarly supports the same conclusion.

Technical Challenges

In contrast to the force restructuring session, participants were provided challenges to consider during the technical challenges session. Participants were asked to focus on the possible implications of these challenges, as well as potential mitigations, in the context of two alternate employment concepts—one represented by the "walk" concept and one represented by the "run" concept depicted in Figure 4.3.

A summary of the challenges, their implications, and potential mitigations for each employment concept is available in a box in Appendix A. In this section, we discuss the top three challenges according to participant prioritization for each employment concept (summarized in Table 4.5), their implications, and potential mitigations.

FIGURE 4.2
Force Restructuring—Average Impact on Operations Versus Average Likelihood

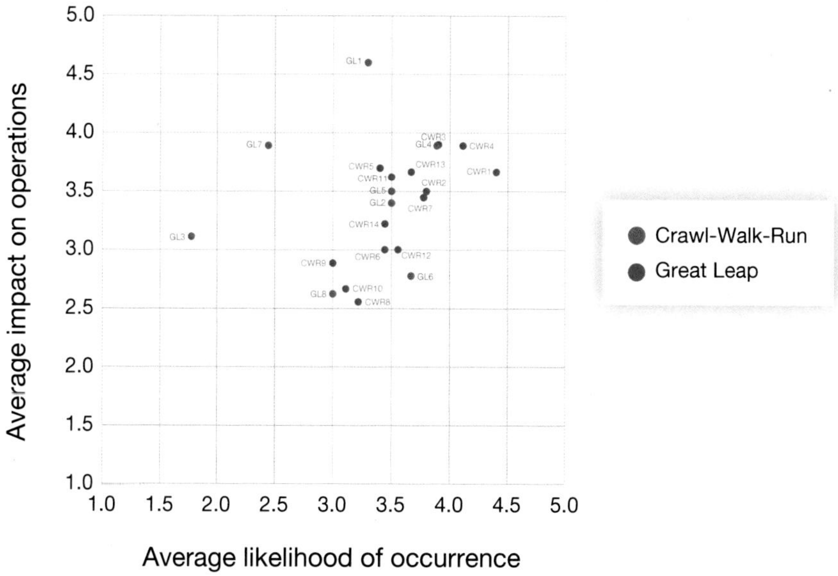

SOURCE: Author analysis of survey results.
NOTE: See Table 4.4 for corresponding graph codes.

Walk

Workshop participants ranked safe operation as the highest-priority challenge for the "walk" employment concept. Beyond concerns over the immediate effects of RL agents or systems pursuing unsafe courses of action, participants also expressed concerns related to who would be responsible if the system went awry. If the RL system had a "hiccup," would the commander still be held responsible? And can commanders still be held responsible if they do not have reliable data? Examples cited involved situations in which schools or other typically "no-strike" targets could shift to or from military uses over time. For instance, a school could be used by an adversary as a munitions depot, or a building that had been used as a munitions depot could have been converted to a school after the adversary redistributed its forces in the region. Accountability would likely fall on a human in the chain of command. If not on the commander, then accountability could potentially fall upon whoever authorized the use of the black box RL technology. Moreover, if the RL system were taken offline because of unsafe operation, then the level of confidence and trust to bring it back online would be difficult to achieve. Participants strongly agreed that, left unmitigated, this challenge could seriously affect operations and national security (mean scores of ~3.8 and ~3.9). Participants also agreed that DoD would have difficulty mitigating its impact (mean score of 3.7).

Potential mitigations included keeping humans in the decision loop in some manner, especially for activities related to target development and weapon allocation. Using multi-

TABLE 4.4
Graph Codes for Figures 4.1 and 4.2

Subsection	Graph Code	Challenge Description
Crawl-Walk-Run	CWR1	DAF and DoD lack workforce to deploy models, such as an ML career field, data cleaning skills
	CWR2	Recruitment and retention of a highly specialized workforce (higher pay outside DoD)
	CWR3	Operators lack training for supervisory control of RL agents or system
	CWR4	Staffing—overbooked, overtasked personnel
	CWR5	Atrophy of battle planning workforce skill
	CWR6	Leadership transformation: manage the culture, change management process, and paint vision for workforce
	CWR7	User adoption may take the human more time
	CWR8	Mission certifications (e.g., predeployment trainings prior to going to an AOC, maintaining training certifications for certain systems)
	CWR9	Cybersecurity certification challenges with administration and training
	CWR10	Morale of the workforce, especially when jobs are at stake (cooperation challenges)
	CWR11	Integration testing is hard (multiple tools to singular gonculator is hard).
	CWR12	Force structure for the workforce
	CWR13	Organization issues: What organization oversees it? Who owns it? Who is the acquisition lead, operations lead, etc.? Is staffing appropriate?
	CWR14	Authorities, security clearance concerns (e.g., AOC at the collateral Secret level, others at various levels. How to oversee the execution of concepts of operation at the right level. Are staff cleared Secret or Top Secret, etc.?)
Great Leap	GL1	No failure mode that is not catastrophic mission failure
	GL2	Lack of trust and understanding of the system
	GL3	Blind trust of the system
	GL4	Less oversight involved and visibility (observability) into when the RL errors are exacerbated by great leap approach.
	GL5	Less reversible than the crawl-walk-run; workforce change is compressed into a short period of time
	GL6	Implications of executing C2 in two different situations or with multiple joint task forces
	GL7	Turning it over to killer robots/RL systems
	GL8	Workforce does not know others' skill sets

FIGURE 4.3
Two Employment Concepts Considered

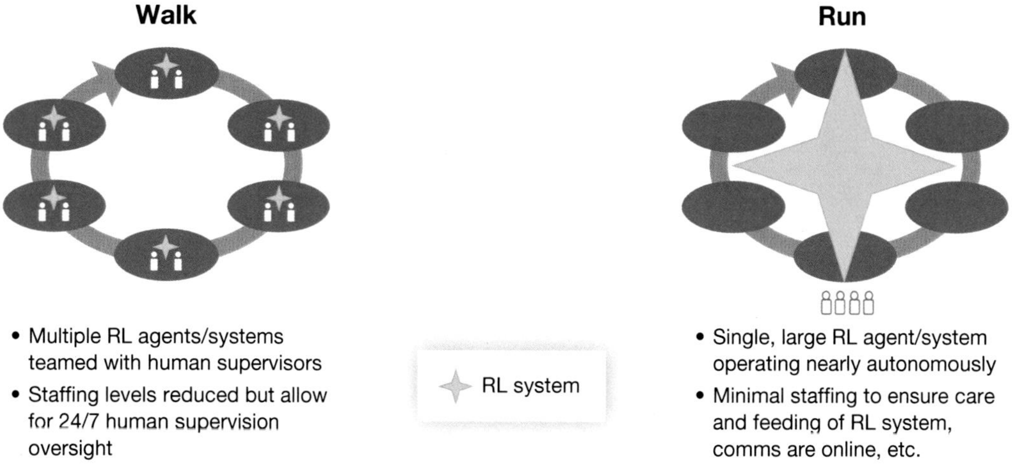

NOTE: Comms – communications.

ple RL agents and selecting courses of action according to some sort of voting scheme (i.e., *ensemble approach*) could also help mitigate this challenge. Some participants suggested that if there were concerns over safe operation for a specific application, then perhaps RL should not be used. The bounds of what is possible with RL and related questions over where it should or should not be used are still being explored. It may be best suited for relatively small, narrow problems.

Identifying the need for retraining was the second highest ranking priority among participants. Participants noted that, in our AOC operational-level C2 example, there may not be enough people with the right skills and expertise or the right processes in place to identify the need in a timely manner. This challenge could be even more difficult if the RL system's performance degraded slowly over time to the extent that its human supervisors would not notice the need—like "boiling a frog." Participants noted that the assessment phase of the ATC (and the joint targeting cycle as well) does not provide instantaneous feedback. It could take 24, 48, or 72 hours to get feedback on how well the campaign is going. Since this feedback is not immediate, it could be difficult to identify the need for retraining, which could in turn magnify the challenge of retraining the system in an operationally relevant time frame. If the system goes awry catastrophically, the need for retraining may be easier to identify, but if the problem is more subtle and manifests more slowly, it could take five or ten days to notice. Making the decision to take the system offline for retraining could be complex, depending on such factors as what fallback options may be available to employ in the meantime. Participants expressed strong agreement that this challenge was likely to occur and difficult to mitigate (mean score of 3.8). Participants also agreed that, left unmitigated, it could have a serious impact on operations (mean score of 3.6).

TABLE 4.5
Top Technical Challenges

	Challenge Description	Priority	Barriers to DoD Detection and Prevention	Other Barriers	Mitigation Difficulty	Impact on Operations	Impact on National Security	Likelihood of Occurrence
Walk	Safe operation (RL can have side effect when pursuing rewards)	1	3.7[a]	3.1	3.5	3.78[b]	3.89[c]	3.5
	Identification of need for retraining; may not happen in time	2	3.5	2.9	3.8[c]	3.6[b]	3.4	3.8[a]
	Incomplete model or response to uncertainty	3	3.33	3	3.33	3.55	3.44	3.56
Run	Modeling is too difficult, or model diverges from reality	1	3.4	3.5	4.1[c]	3.5	3.5	3.8
	Safe operation (RL can have side effect when pursuing rewards)	2	3.78[a]	2.56	3.44	3.78[b]	3.89[c]	3.56
	Identification of need for retraining	3	3.2	2.6	3.4	3.5	3.4	3.6

SOURCE: Author analysis of survey results.

NOTE: Evaluation statements were scored on a scale from strongly disagree (1) to strongly agree (5). Numbers shown represent the mean taken from ten completed participant surveys.

[a] *p*-value at or above the 95-percent confidence interval.

[b] *p*-value at or above the 98-percent confidence interval.

[c] *p*-value at or above the 99-percent confidence interval.

Potential mitigations discussed included implementing some type of oversight by knowledgeable people and defining a set of parameters that, if exceeded, are flagged by the system. Another possibility involved having a well-defined set of tasks that the RL agent or system is trained to do and setting appropriate limits on its activities. For example, if an RL system is used for route planning and a new surface-to-air missile with greater range and speed is deployed, the RL system could be declared no longer certified for use.

The third highest priority challenge deals with the use of incomplete models for training RL agents and how these agents respond to uncertainty. The greatest strength and weakness of RL is its ability to cover a whole "decision surface." This capability makes it attractive to some but a cause for concern to others. Participants generally agreed that this challenge was likely to occur (3.56) and have a serious impact on operations and national security if left unmitigated (3.55 and 3.44, respectively).

One potential mitigation is pursuing additional research and development to find the "right problem" on which to use RL. Another related approach is judicious selection of applications of RL. If there is a closed-form analytic solution to the problem at hand, then it should be used, if time allows. RL may not provide an optimal solution, but it could provide a useful solution to use in situations in which there is not enough time to use more-traditional methods. RL should be viewed as one tool in a suite of tools, not necessarily as a substitute for existing or more-traditional tools and methods.

Run

The top two technical challenges from the "walk" employment concept—safe operation and identifying the need for retraining—also appear in the top three for the "run" employment concept, ranked second and third, respectively, by participants in terms of priority. The top prioritized challenge for the "run" employment concept involves the problem of the environment being too difficult to model and/or model divergence from reality. Interestingly, this challenge leapt to the top of the list for workshop participants for the "run" employment concept from its sixth-place ranking for the "walk" employment concept. Should this challenge arise, then the RL system could wind up as an ineffective tool that does not address the real-world problem for which it is needed. Participants strongly agreed that this challenge was likely to occur (3.8) and that it would be difficult for DoD to mitigate (mean score of 4.1).

A potential mitigation approach is to train RL agents with a broad environment (or even a broad range of environments). For a narrow application, such as training an RL agent to route an aircraft around radars, this could translate into including a wider variety of radars in the environment than would be expected to be encountered in reality for some portion of the agent's training and then focusing on the known or expected radars for the remainder. Participants noted that this could be a difficult and potentially time-consuming process. Nation-state–level resources could help ameliorate these issues, at least for relatively narrow applications. Applying this approach to a broad application, such as the one envisioned in the "run" employment concept, may not be feasible.

Additional Discussions

At the end of the workshop, time was devoted to discussing additional issues that may have come from a larger perspective gained from the previous sessions. The following is a summary of the feedback:

1. The challenge to the workforce continued to be of primary concern and is multidimensional in nature. Training the workforce with highly sought specialized skills in the commercial sector, with no viable path to retention, is a recipe for failure. Further, the participants were concerned that current personnel would be expected to take on additional RL-related tasks without having proper incentives in place to support these tasks.

2. Deficiencies in addressing workforce size and training could spill over into deficiencies in identifying problems in RL operation and the need for retraining the system. If RL performance deficiencies were incremental in nature, for example, the attention needed to recognize such problems might be lacking, or the type and frequency might not clearly signal the need to retrain. Assessing the performance and getting authorization to retrain might be delayed, and retraining might not happen soon enough or become infeasible, especially if problems occur during a mission.
3. Data use and classification may be problematic. Not everyone is using data the same way, and standards do not exist. Some data may be highly classified, whereas operational personnel may not be cleared to access the source data directly. The RL would train on it, however, and it might be challenging to overcome classification and the ability to oversee and judge the correct operation of the RL.
4. There is a potential problem in becoming "locked in" to these RL systems that could limit the ability to pursue other solutions in the future. This could be a greater issue for the Great Leap than for Crawl-Walk-Run.
5. Cost and benefit that the commercial world is seeing seem almost out of whack for DoD at this stage. Companies have spent billions on AI without a clear profit.

CHAPTER 5

Conclusions and Recommendations

This chapter summarizes some of the primary conclusions from the previous chapters.

- Many of the primary challenges to using RL in DoD are not particular to RL but rather are more general, including lack of workforce skill needed for developing, fielding, and assessing AI applications. Further, the commercial sector pays high premiums for skills centered on machine intelligence, and the inability to attract and retain such skills may preclude large-scale DoD development, as is currently happening in industry.
- RL is an approach to training an agent and not a single technology. Many implementation variations exist, each having different trade-offs. The wide range of implementation, the empirical nature of the field, and the black box nature of RL decisionmaking do not lend themselves to a comprehensive, analytical approach to evaluating what DoD applications would benefit the most from RL. Many high-profile successes (e.g., beating world experts in game play) exact little consequence for *mission failure* (i.e., losing the game), whereas in DoD applications, such consequences could be considerable. The use of other, more-established technologies may provide a better performance-risk ratio in some cases.
- RL is a data-intensive technology whose training needs grow with the size of the problem. Datasets need to cover sufficient variations in the environment in which the RL operates to prevent unanticipated or undesired behavior. Depending on the application and how RL is used, this may be a limitation difficult for DoD to overcome. In the case of autonomous driving, for example, large sets of good decision data could be collected as drivers navigated roads in a range of situations. For a broad, decision-based application, there may be too few high-level decisions to effectively train an RL, and they may not cover all expected situations.
- The threshold at which an RL system needs additional training is not clear. The mantra that "more training data are needed" seems to be the solution for an ad hoc approach to failure based on observing behavior that deviates from our own intuition. We do not know exactly when an RL system will fail, nor can we predict how it will fail with precision. Thus, both identifying what constitutes a failure that warrants retraining and gauging the potential frequency of failure are problematic.
- Trust issues and the inability to judge misbehavior may also limit the size of an RL application. Intermediate outputs that could be generated from narrow uses of RL are more

likely to have outputs within the ability of current personnel to evaluate. Leveraging RL for broad applications having large, diverse volumes of input data to make decisions would likely be beyond the capabilities of a human to effectively oversee.
- A failure in RL for a broad application, such as the operational-level C2 example considered in our workshop, may mean catastrophic mission failure. Moreover, taking a system offline may not be an option when personnel may no longer be in place to take over or the skills of remaining personnel have atrophied.

Recommendations

- DoD should explore ways to attract, train, and retain the skill sets needed in AI. It is unrealistic to assume that any broad RL applications can be developed, tested, deployed, and maintained without sustained access to expertise in data science, modeling and simulation, ML and RL algorithm development, and other skills needed. Furthermore, just as the workforce adapted to the rise of technology in the workplace, DoD forces will need to adapt to leveraging AI in many everyday decisionmaking activities. Given that progress and change are currently so rapid, it may be less valuable to specify a list of skills than it is to require continuous adaptation to the rapidly changing technology landscape of AI. In many cases, AI can be viewed as another technology to supplement existing skills and experience. While leveraging external expertise is likely necessary, as with industrial, academic, and FFRDC partners, too much dependence on external expertise and development could risk vendor lock for larger RL applications. Such dependence on particular vendors can arise from proprietary RL algorithm development, training recipes, or even proprietary datasets. In contrast, where feasible, DoD should view the existing force structure as a valuable asset to aid the development of AI, especially in the verification and validation process.
- DoD should develop ways to access and generate high-quality data relevant to DoD problems and required in training for RL algorithms. This recommendation can be broken into several areas:
  - *Existing data.* Diversity in data types, formats, classification, and even utility can vary across DoD. As RL training requirements can grow considerably with respect to application complexity and performance improvements, constrained data access may become the limiting factor for an RL application.
  - *Data difficult to capture, too sparse in nature, or subject to deep uncertainty.* One issue with training a broad, decision-based application may be that there may not be enough existing data to train on or the means to generate it. For example, a commander's decisions, even if recorded, likely cannot be collected in the volumes needed to serve as example data to train an RL system, especially in response to RL exploration. Simulating everything needed for an RL system to explore and learn may be intractable computationally. Deep unknowns may not be captured. In such cases, it

may be necessary to draw on more-analytic approaches or approaches that draw on decisionmaking in the face of deep uncertainty.[1] These may supplement an RL system or be used to create decisional data in response to RL actions and against which an RL system can train. Low-probability, high-impact events were shown to be problematic for autonomous driving. A shadow cast on the road or an unexpected pedestrian might be misinterpreted and cause the system to veer off course—or might even go unrecognized. Determining ways to collect or generate relevant training data for such cases is especially relevant in DoD applications in which such events may be especially significant.

- *Real-world data as close to operational as is feasible.* Because RL-trained systems are sensitive to distributional shifts in the environment, the system needs to train with real data at some point. Training under enough real-world examples, as is done in autonomous driving, may be a limiting factor in the use of RL for many applications.
- *Dynamic data generated to train against problematic cases uncovered during testing and evaluation (T&E) or to make the RL system more robust against unanticipated challenges.* RL learns through extensive exploration, but it can be impractical to ensure that a system is exposed to enough real-world situations to guarantee safe operation. DoD may explore several paths to help with this. First, T&E should not be considered separate from training. Data collected during T&E, especially around failure cases, can be used to generate training examples for RL. Second, generative AI might be leveraged to present more-realistic test cases for training in response to RL exploration. Third, adversarial AI may be useful for finding challenges difficult to anticipate and training RL to respond to them.

• Before DoD can likely leverage the advantages of RL, it should better understand the limits of RL application and how RL provides an advantage over existing technology. Several areas of development could aid in this understanding:
  - A risk framework for RL would be of value for guiding which applications may present too high a risk in relation to expected benefits. Lack of domain generalization and domain size and computational feasibility challenges (Chapter 2) both conspire to make failure rates and failure modes unpredictable. RL may be especially prone to such failure uncertainties given that it learns from interaction with the environment, which does not always include some exploration that may be unsafe or in unanticipated environments—and thus a complete statistical failure rate may be left uncharacterized. In other complex software systems, operational usage is sufficient to generate failure statistics, and the approach of development is to compartmentalize functionality. The approach with current models is to grow neural net size and use the neural net's unconstrained behavior to learn from interaction. Such an approach does not necessarily limit behavior in the same fashion as in conventional software

[1] Vincent A. W. J. Marchau, Warren E. Walker, Pieter J. T. M. Bloemen, and Steven W. Popper, *Decision Making Under Deep Uncertainty: From Theory to Practice*, Springer Nature, 2019.

applications, whose behavior is deterministic and built from smaller blocks of code to purposely limit side effects. Such differences should be considered in determining acceptable risk as the models grow in size. Consideration of which potential risks are acceptable or able to be sufficiently mitigated would inform such applications.

- The uncertainty in decisionmaking (*unexplainability*) needs to be better bounded regarding the type and likelihood of failure. In lieu of *explainable AI* (i.e., systems whose decisions are explainable—and possibly predictable—by humans), we may be left with systems that always require strong mitigation measures to prevent catastrophic consequences. Such measures would likely confine the employment of RL to narrow applications in which negative consequences are limited or human intervention is able to prevent such consequences.
- DoD should explore how and when to develop trust in systems whose behavior is not explainable. We already place trust in technological systems that behave in inexplicable ways. Software, in its many forms, runs many systems and fails in inexplicable ways. We also trust it to run many critical systems, and it provides many perceived advantages. A better means to determine when a system warrants trust and how to develop it would aid in determining which applications may be amenable to the use of RL.
- A methodology should be developed to discern, among all the different types of RL, their trade-offs in risk, performance, cost, and other measures and how they best compete with and work in tandem with other technologies. Such a methodology needs to address all challenges a DoD application would present to a target system. The current approach of presenting an algorithm that purports to solve one RL challenge (e.g., safe behavior or reward hacking) and ignore others does not lend itself to evaluating RL algorithms against the simultaneous complex challenges in a DoD scenario.
- DoD should explore what key data features are needed to train an RL system to reduce data demands. Our tendency to anthropomorphize AI behavior, coupled with its seemingly inexplicable behavior, may indicate that we fundamentally misunderstand how RL learns. Our assumption that RL systems learn as biological systems do is founded, at best, on a crude representation of a small portion of a brain and, at worst, fails to capture essential elements of learning in biological systems. While an odd behavior in RL may indicate the need for more training data, it may also indicate that we have failed to understand what features RL learns from. An analogy is that we can understand cartoon representations of the world that are greatly reduced in complexity. If we can greatly reduce the data needed to train RL, we may be able to train larger applications through greater permutations to reduce unexpected failure.

• DoD should consider where incremental advances can be leveraged into bigger solutions. Progress in the field of gaming, for example, did not appear suddenly. Further, algorithms were tailored to the type of problem and computational resources available. The resulting systems often bested the best players, and they could be used to train even better systems. Given the current limitations of DoD, an incremental approach may result in gains in performance without some of the risks of pursuing a broad application for gains that have not been justified. Further, such systems may be leveraged to train larger, higher-performing RL systems.

- One example to which DoD can apply this approach is the ATC of Figure 3.1. While a comprehensive development plan is beyond the scope of this report, DoD may want to consider the following suggestions:
  - Perform a cost, benefit, and risk analysis of existing processes of the ATC to determine the best technology solutions to each subprocess. Some subprocesses may be best improved with specialized AI or even with non-AI solutions. For example, image recognition algorithms are well developed using ML, and they would likely be part of the target development process in Figure 3.1.
  - Develop the resulting technologies to complement and support the existing force structure. This approach carries several advantages: First, it leverages the existing expertise within the AOC to serve as feedback to the developers of the technology; second, it can serve as a mechanism for T&E to ensure that the resulting technology functions as expected; third, it reduces risk to the overall ATC because technology transition can be more finely controlled.
  - Develop approaches for process validation and data sharing among the elements of the AOC and ATC. AI differs from humans in both its decision process and the data used for making decisions. ML and RL can process large datasets to create information interpretable by humans, but such information is not necessarily ideal for sharing between blocks of the ATC process. As the larger ATC process is pieced together with information flowing between blocks (Figure 3.1), DoD can explore what information is useful for the decisionmaking process of the technology and what is useful for the force elements that both leverage the technology and serve to validate its functionality.
  - Explore the use of RL and other AI methods for use in the final decisionmaking process in the ATC under sparse input data and uncertain outcomes. Several challenges need to be overcome to use RL as it is currently done: First, the current ATC results from human decisions that do not provide the volume of input data and examples needed to effectively train RL. Second, RL needs to explore the consequences of various AODs resulting from the ATC (refer to Figure 3.1). These consequences may be difficult to predict with great certainty, and, furthermore, they may be shaped by deep uncertainties within data used to formulate the AODs. In such cases, the RL needs to be able to identify the limits of its predictive capability and to generate decisions according to predetermined conservative courses of action.

Final Thoughts

RL, and AI in general, offers DoD attractive capabilities with potential strategic advantages. Such technology is challenged by the broad nature of many DoD missions, especially those that might involve strategic decisionmaking. Because RL learns through repeated interactions with its environment, such missions can resist the simulation that would provide RL with sufficient training examples under enough conditions to prevent potentially catastrophic failure to the mission. Since RL has demonstrated incredible capabilities in solving narrow problems, the value to DoD might be in finding the "sweet spot" in DoD missions, where RL can be trained sufficiently to supplement or exceed the decisionmaking capabilities of humans while its failures are sufficiently mitigated to reduce mission risk to acceptable levels. In tandem, it is important to consider risks arising solely from technical failure. Important also are impacts to force structure and ability to train, operate, and maintain any RL-based system. Skilled personnel may be needed to mitigate potential RL failures or remain in place to monitor and assess RL output. Lost skills, skill degradation, personnel displacement, and the need for specialized AI-related skills are all factors to consider in choosing where RL provides the most value to DoD.

APPENDIX A

Additional Workshop Details

Workshop Format

We convened 11 experts from the Army, Air Force, and RAND in a workshop to identify challenges to employing RL in a complex military scenario (see box below and Table A.1). Five RAND team members and two government representatives of our sponsor also supported throughout the exercise but were not asked to provide evaluations. We asked participants to identify those challenges' implications and potential mitigation strategies that can used to overcome the challenges. At the end of the workshop, participants then ranked and evaluated the challenges according to several statements (Table A.2).

Expert Elicitation Workshop Approach

Exploratory discussion	Semistructured discussion to elicit challenges associated with force restructuring and technical areas *"Given the complex military scenario presented, what are some challenges that could arise?"*
Qualitative analysis	Analysis of content from the exploratory discussion
Implication and mitigation strategy elicitation	Open discussion to elicit the implications and potential mitigation strategies associated with each identified challenge *"What are the implications of this particular challenge?"* *"How could DoD mitigate this challenge?"*
Challenge evaluation	Closed-ended survey to evaluate challenges based on evaluation statements Rank challenge priorities 1 to *N*
Quantitative analysis	Challenge rankings and statistical significance

SOURCE: Adapted from Mayer et al., 2021.

TABLE A.1
Workshop Participant Backgrounds

Participant Membership	Total Participants	Total Evaluations
U.S. Air Force	5	5
U.S. Army	2	2
RAND SMEs	4	3
RAND study team	5	—
Government sponsor	2	—
Total	18	10

NOTE: SMEs = subject-matter experts.

TABLE A.2
Evaluation Statements and Definitions

Evaluation Statement	Definition
Barriers to DoD detection and prevention	DoD is unlikely to detect this challenge prior to it being realized or to prevent it from being realized even if it is detected (e.g., because of a lack of ability or willingness, or other barriers).
Other barriers	Other than barriers to DoD detection and prevention, there are very few barriers that could keep this challenge from being realized (barriers may include, e.g., lack of technology readiness or adversary ability or intent to adopt technology, forces that change external factors, U.S. institutional or cultural incentives).
Mitigation difficulty	If this challenge is realized, it will be difficult for DoD to mitigate its impact (e.g., through authorities, capability, knowledge, costs, effort, time).
Impact on operations	Left unmitigated, this challenge will severely limit (directly or indirectly) DoD's options for performing operations.
Impact on national security	Left unmitigated, this challenge will severely negatively affect (directly or indirectly) U.S. national security (e.g., via changes to economy, culture, politics, military operations).
Likelihood of occurrence	This challenge is likely to occur given the scenario presented.

SOURCE: Adapted from Mayer et al., 2021.

APPENDIX B

Challenges, Implications, and Mitigation Strategies Identified in the Workshop

Table B.1 summarizes the force restructuring and technical challenges, implications, and mitigation strategies identified in the workshop.

TABLE B.1

Challenges Identified

Challenge Category	Challenge Title and/or Description	Implications	Mitigation Strategy
	Crawl-Walk-Run		
Force restructuring	DAF and DoD lack workforce to deploy models, such as an ML career field, data cleaning skills	Army: Eggs all in one basket for Palantir system. Unsure of what all it can and cannot do. Outsourcing of the capability. "Trust us, the magic box works." Loss of control. Reliant on nongovernment entity (contractor).	Civilian workforce, expanded engineering series, use of FFRDCs, warrant officer program
	Staffing—overbooked, overtasked personnel	Testing, care, feeding overlooked	Expand size of the workforce
	User adoption may take the human more time	The RL is not used or is turned off. Disuse.	Training, user-friendliness, required usage, divestiture from legacy systems
	Morale of the workforce, especially when jobs are at stake (cooperation challenges)	People leave the military, get discouraged; increased risk of insider threats	Be transparent in executing the plan as stated; reshape the force; incentivize with new opportunities (e.g., training, "Shark Tank"–style innovation competition)
	Atrophy of battle planning workforce skill	If system goes offline, workforce lacks skills for battle planning	Adaptive automation so human planners still have responsibility (reduce skill atrophy)

Table B.1—Continued

Challenge Category	Challenge Title and/or Description	Implications	Mitigation Strategy
Force restructuring	Integration testing is hard (multiple tools to singular "gonculator" is hard).		
	Leadership transformation; manage the culture, manage the change process, and paint vision for workforce	Cynicism, lack of full user adoption, morale problems, high turnover	Leadership (generals) from nonoperations career field
	Operators lack training for supervisory control of RL agents or system.	The system does not work effectively.	Training staff and supervisors
	Cybersecurity certification challenges with administration and training	Limited access controls, increased vulnerability, potential separation of responsibilities (compliance concerns)	Build the system such that operators do not need elevated access to the systems (i.e., write in contracts)
	Force structure for the workforce	Reduction in capacity; do less of it, or it is altogether eliminated	
	Recruitment and retention of a highly specialized workforce (higher pay outside DoD)	Insufficient workforce to execute the plan	Special incentive pay; active-duty service commitment; operating in real-world problems (sense of mission); change of enlistment standards; lateral entry of workforce into higher grade instead of beginning at O-1 grade
	Mission certifications (e.g., predeployment trainings prior to going to an AOC or maintaining training certifications for certain systems)	Personnel rotating to an AOC lack familiarity with a system, lack of training on new system	Include the training in formal training unit; in the AOC itself, there are organic training assets for individuals rotating in
	Authorities, security clearance concerns (e.g., AOC at the collateral Secret level, others at various levels: How to oversee the execution of concepts of operation at the right level? Are staff cleared Secret or Top Secret, etc.?)	Operator at AOC may have only partial access, system must deal with data at multiple levels or gets bumped to higher classification, security and insider threat vulnerabilities increase	Align clearance levels; upgrade clearances; create intermediary system with piecemeal or modular approach

Table B.1—Continued

Challenge Category	Challenge Title and/or Description	Implications	Mitigation Strategy
		Great Leap	
Force restructuring	No failure mode that is not catastrophic mission failure	Catastrophic mission failure	Run a parallel AOC at the same time, and develop trust that AI AOC is doing the right thing and being useful; geographically separate AOC as reach-back capability not being run by RL piece; exercise this practice
	Lack of trust and understanding of the system		
	Blind trust in the system		
	Implications of executing C2 in two different situations or with multiple joint task forces	Lack of flexibility; things are centralized and you need multiple skill sets	
	Less reversible than the crawl-walk-run; workforce change is compressed into a short period	Difficult to get to high skill level; tough to absorb personnel in time span required	Retain past retirement; change tenure; provide waivers; use a system that rolls out less rapidly; consider robustness and resilience perspective.
	Less oversight involved and visibility (observability) into when the RL errs are exacerbated by great leap approach	Poor mission performance	RL provides list of multiple possible courses of action, and humans adjudicate; skeleton crew has authority to make decisions.
	Workforce does not know others' skill sets		
	Turning it over to killer robots or RL systems	Lack of humans to evaluate the plan	Keep humans in the loop
		Walk Phase	
Technical	Identifying need for retraining; may not be possible in time	May not have the right people or processes in place to identify the need; may not notice slow decline in "boiling frog effect"; may have to take offline if something new arises	Oversight by SMEs/ knowledgeable people; parameters that the system flags when they are exceeded; well-defined set of tasks to train that RL can fall back on if needed > RL no longer certified for use

Table B.1—Continued

Challenge Category	Challenge Title and/or Description	Implications	Mitigation Strategy
Technical	Retraining feasibility (Can we afford to retrain? Do we take offline?)	Need for mission risk assessment if taking the system offline; need to consider speed or length of time to retrain with implications to mission; option to accept risk and keep online; retraining may not work as expected, causing system degradation	Gather consensus from SMEs/senior leaders; use ensembles of models (not just a single agent but hundreds with several models to choose from) to buy time back; acquire more computing resources to retrain quicker
	Too difficult to model or model diverges from reality (people in place may not be able to explain or use features); there is divergence on which data to use (and they are updated at different times)	A useless and ineffective tool that does not do what it is needed for in the real world, one that degrades performance	Train with broad cross-section of what may be encountered (e.g., to train an aircraft to avoid radar, train with wide variety of radars present in reality)
	Lack of explainability (RL systems built from neural nets are black boxes)	Cannot ask system how it came to the conclusion that it did; implications for frequency of training; trade-offs with importance of explainability	Build a level of trust with system and commander; take an iterative approach to replacing human tasks with AI/RL ones; train iteratively; build explanation interface into the system; train on features that humans recognize (i.e., that are more human-interpretable) (train on human performance data); require the system to explain certain things when risk is high enough (e.g., if bombing a former school turned weapon depot)
	Safe operation (RL can have side effects when pursuing rewards)	Accountability for actions taken by AI—is the commander responsible? Commanders and decisionmakers may distrust if collateral damage is a possibility; the standard may be higher for a system in terms of justifying risk of harm.	Keep a human in the loop with ability to say "no" or do something different; use an ensemble approach with multiple options up for a vote; do not let RL solve this problem in the first place (if of high-enough risk and no safe way to do it); perform alternative analyses for better ways to solve problem

Table B.1—Continued

Challenge Category	Challenge Title and/or Description	Implications	Mitigation Strategy
Technical	Incomplete model or response to uncertainty	Presents advantage for RL (but also a weakness)	Quantify the advantages versus potential disadvantages; more research
	Reward hacking	Lack of gut reactions that the human element has (how to get the system to mimic that)	Ensure in contract that the AI does not behave perversely or do things we do not want; training; have a range of models for the range of possible scenarios
	Adversarial attack (adversary exploits failure mode in RL operation; poor data, input, or training information)	No quick solution to systematic failure; upstream failure; problem is difficult to catch	Backup solutions; may have to rethink system
	Run Phase		
Technical	Identifying need for retraining	May not have the right people or processes in the places to identify the need; may not notice slow decline in "boiling frog effect"; may have to take offline if something new arises	Oversight by SMEs/knowledgeable people; parameters that the system flags when they are exceeded; well-defined set of tasks to train that RL can fall back on if needed > RL no longer certified for use
	Retraining feasibility (can we afford to retrain? Do we take offline?)	Need for mission risk assessment if taking the system offline; need to consider speed or length of time to retrain with implications to mission; option to accept risk and keep online; retraining may not work as expected, causing system degradation	Gather consensus from SMEs/senior leaders; use ensembles of models (not just a single agent but hundreds with several models to choose from) to buy time back; acquire more computing resources to retrain quicker

Table B.1—Continued

Challenge Category	Challenge Title and/or Description	Implications	Mitigation Strategy
Technical	Too difficult to model or model diverges from reality	A useless and ineffective tool that does not do what it is needed for in the real world; one that degrades performance	Train with broad cross-section of what may be encountered (e.g., to train an aircraft to avoid radar, train with wide variety of radars present in reality)
	Lack of explainability (RL systems built from neural nets are black boxes)	Cannot ask system how it came to the conclusion that it did; implications for frequency of training; trade-offs with importance of explainability	Build a level of trust with system and commander; take an iterative approach to replacing human tasks with AI/RL ones; train iteratively; build explanation interface into the system; train on features that humans recognize (i.e., that are more human-interpretable) (train on human performance data); require the system to explain certain things when risk is high enough (e.g., if bombing a former school turned weapon depot)
	Safe operation (RL can have side effects when pursuing rewards)	Accountability for actions taken by AI—is the commander responsible? Commanders and decisionmakers may distrust if collateral damage is a possibility; the standard may be higher for a system in terms of justifying risk of harm.	Keep a human in the loop with ability to say "no" or do something different; use an ensemble approach with multiple options up for a vote; do not let RL solve this problem in the first place (if of high-enough risk and no safe way to do it); perform alternative analyses for better ways to solve problem
	Incomplete model or response to uncertainty	Presents advantage for RL (but also a weakness)	Quantify the advantages versus potential disadvantages; more research
	Reward hacking	Lack of gut reactions that the human element has (how to get the system to mimic that)	Ensure in contract that the AI does not behave perversely or do things we do not want; training; have a range of models for the range of possible scenarios
	Adversarial attack (adversary exploits failure mode in RL operation)	No quick solution to systematic failure; upstream failure; problem is difficult to catch	Backup solutions; may have to rethink system

Abbreviations

AI	artificial intelligence
AOC	air operations center
AOD	air operations directive
ATC	air tasking cycle
ATO	air tasking order
C2	command and control
DAF	Department of the Air Force
DL	deep learning
DNN	deep neural network
DoD	Department of Defense
FFRDC	federally funded research and development center
IL	imitation learning
JFACC	joint forces air component commander
ML	machine learning
NAS	Neural Architecture Search
ORL	offline reinforcement learning
RL	reinforcement learning
/s	per second
SME	subject-matter expert
T&E	testing and evaluation

References

Adami, Christoph, "A Brief History of Artificial Intelligence Research," *Artificial Life*, Vol. 27, No. 2, 2021.

Agarwal, Alekh, Sarah Bird, Markus Cozowicz, Luong Hoang, John Langford, Stephen Lee, Jiaji Li, Dan Melamed, Gal Oshri, and Oswaldo Ribas, "Making Contextual Decisions with Low Technical Debt," arXiv preprint arXiv:1606.03966, 2016.

Amodei, Dario, Chris Olah, Jacob Steinhardt, Paul Christiano, John Schulman, and Dan Mané, "Concrete Problems in AI Safety," arXiv preprint arXiv:1606.06565, 2016.

Ananthaswamy, Anil, "DeepMind AI Topples Experts at Complex Game Stratego," *Nature*, December 1, 2022.

Aptiv, "Autonomous Mobility," webpage, undated. As of October 6, 2023: https://www.aptiv.com/en/solutions/autonomous-mobility

Baert, Mattijs, Sam Leroux, and Pieter Simoens, "Inverse Reinforcement Learning Through Logic Constraint Inference," *Machine Learning*, Vol. 112, 2023.

Balduzzi, David, Marta Garnelo, Yoram Bachrach, Wojciech Czarnecki, Julien Perolat, Max Jaderberg, and Thore Graepel, "Open-Ended Learning in Symmetric Zero-Sum Games," *Proceedings of the International Conference on Machine Learning*, 2019.

Baldwin, Robert, "Self-Driving-Car Research Has Cost $16 Billion. What Do We Have to Show for It?" *Car and Driver*, February 10, 2020.

Bansal, Mayank, and Abhijit Ogale, "Learning to Drive: Beyond Pure Imitation," *Waypoint* blog, Waymo, December 10, 2018. As of September 28, 2023: https://blog.waymo.com/2019/08/learning-to-drive-beyond-pure-imitation_26.html

Bar-Hillel, Maya, and Avishai Margalit, "How Vicious Are Cycles of Intransitive Choice?" *Theory and Decision*, Vol. 24, 1988.

Bengio, Yoshua, Yann Lecun, and Geoffrey Hinton, "Deep Learning for AI," *Communications of the ACM*, Association for Computing Machinery, Vol. 64, No. 7, 2021.

Berner, Christopher, Greg Brockman, Brooke Chan, Vicki Cheung, Przemysław Dębiak, Christy Dennison, David Farhi, Quirin Fischer, Shariq Hashme, and Chris Hesse, "Dota 2 with Large Scale Deep Reinforcement Learning," arXiv preprint arXiv:1912.06680, 2019.

Biggio, Battista, and Fabio Roli, "Wild Patterns: Ten Years After the Rise of Adversarial Machine Learning," *Pattern Recognition*, Vol. 84, December 1, 2018.

Bokonda, P. L., K. Ouazzani-Touhami, and N. Souissi, "Predictive Analysis Using Machine Learning: Review of Trends and Methods," *Proceedings of the 2020 International Symposium on Advanced Electrical and Communication Technologies (ISAECT)*, 2020.

Boloor, A., X. He, C. Gill, Y. Vorobeychik, and X. Zhang, "Simple Physical Adversarial Examples Against End-to-End Autonomous Driving Models," *Proceedings of the 2019 IEEE International Conference on Embedded Software and Systems (ICESS)*, 2019.

Borne, Kyle David, "Targeting in Multi-Domain Operations," *Military Review*, Vol. 99, 2019.

Bory, Paolo, "Deep New: The Shifting Narratives of Artificial Intelligence from Deep Blue to AlphaGo," *Convergence*, Vol. 25, No. 4, 2019.

Brown, Chris, "Waymo Outlines Plans to Integrate Autonomous Trucking in Fleets," *Fleet Forward*, July 14, 2020.

Burch, Neil, "Time and Space: Why Imperfect Information Games Are Hard," thesis, University of Alberta, 2018.

Burmeister, J., and J. Wiles, "The Challenge of Go as a Domain for AI Research: A Comparison Between Go and Chess," *Proceedings of Third Australian and New Zealand Conference on Intelligent Information Systems*, 1995.

Buttazzo, G., "Artificial Consciousness: Utopia or Real Possibility?" *Computer*, Vol. 34, No. 7, 2001.

Campbell, Murray, "Knowledge Discovery in Deep Blue," *Communications of the ACM*, Association for Computing Machinery, Vol. 42, No. 11, 1999.

Carlström, Niclas, "Enhancement of Radar Tracking with Low Level Radar Data," briefing slides, Aptiv, November 2019.

Carnegie Mellon University Audiovisual Center, "Research Themes," webpage, Carnegie Mellon University Robotics Institute, undated. As of October 6, 2023: https://labs.ri.cmu.edu/argo-ai-center/research/

Cason, Timothy N., Daniel Friedman, and E. D. Hopkins, "Cycles and Instability in a Rock-Paper-Scissors Population Game: A Continuous Time Experiment," *Review of Economic Studies*, Vol. 81, No. 1, 2014.

Chen, Lili, Kevin Lu, Aravind Rajeswaran, Kimin Lee, Aditya Grover, Misha Laskin, Pieter Abbeel, Aravind Srinivas, and Igor Mordatch, "Decision Transformer: Reinforcement Learning via Sequence Modeling," *Advances in Neural Information Processing Systems*, Vol. 34, 2021.

Chen, Minmin, Alex Beutel, Paul Covington, Sagar Jain, Francois Belletti, and Ed H. Chi, "Top-K Off-Policy Correction for a REINFORCE Recommender System," *Proceedings of the Twelfth ACM International Conference on Web Search and Data Mining*, 2019.

Cheng, Shuyang, Yang Song, and Peisheng Li, "Using Automated Data Augmentation to Advance Our Waymo Driver," *Waypoint* blog, Waymo, April 2, 2020. As of September 28, 2023: https://blog.waymo.com/2020/04/using-automated-data-augmentation-to.html

Cobbe, Karl, Oleg Klimov, Chris Hesse, Taehoon Kim, and John Schulman, "Quantifying Generalization in Reinforcement Learning," *Proceedings of the International Conference on Machine Learning*, 2019.

Costa, Diogo M., "Computational Complexity of Games and Puzzles," master's thesis, Harvard University, July 2018.

Cubuk, Ekin Dogus, and Barret Zoph, "Improving Deep Learning Performance with AutoAugment," Google Research blog, June 4, 2018. As of October 9, 2023: https://ai.googleblog.com/2018/06/improving-deep-learning-performance.html

Cubuk, Ekin D., Barret Zoph, Jonathon Shlens, and Quoc V. Le, "RandAugment: Practical Automated Data Augmentation with a Reduced Search Space," version 2, arXiv preprint arXiv:1909.13719, November 14, 2019.

Czarnecki, Wojciech M., Gauthier Gidel, Brendan Tracey, Karl Tuyls, Shayegan Omidshafiei, David Balduzzi, and Max Jaderberg, "Real World Games Look Like Spinning Tops," *Advances in Neural Information Processing Systems*, Vol. 33, 2020.

Das, A., V. Shroff, A. Jain, and G. Sharma, "Knowledge Transfer Between Similar Atari Games Using Deep Q-Networks to Improve Performance," *Proceedings of the 12th International Conference on Computing Communication and Networking Technologies (ICCCNT)*, 2021.

Daskalakis, Constantinos, Noah Golowich, and Kaiqing Zhang, "The Complexity of Markov Equilibrium in Stochastic Games," unpublished manuscript, April 2022.

Demontis, Ambra, Maura Pintor, Luca Demetrio, Kathrin Grosse, Hsiao-Ying Lin, Chengfang Fang, Battista Biggio, and Fabio Roli, "A Survey on Reinforcement Learning Security with Application to Autonomous Driving," arXiv preprint arXiv:2212.06123, 2022.

Desislavov, Radosvet, Fernando Martínez-Plumed, and José Hernández-Orallo, "Compute and Energy Consumption Trends in Deep Learning Inference," arXiv preprint arXiv:2109.05472, 2021.

Dike, H. U., Y. Zhou, K. K. Deveerasetty, and Q. Wu, "Unsupervised Learning Based on Artificial Neural Network: A Review," *Proceedings of the 2018 IEEE International Conference on Cyborg and Bionic Systems*, 2018.

Dong, Hao, Zihan Ding, and Shanghang Zhang, *Deep Reinforcement Learning: Fundamentals, Research and Application*, Springer, 2020.

Došilović, F. K., M. Brčić, and N. Hlupić, "Explainable Artificial Intelligence: A Survey," *Proceedings of the 41st International Convention on Information and Communication Technology, Electronics and Microelectronics (MIPRO)*, 2018.

Du, Simon S., Sham M. Kakade, Ruosong Wang, and Lin F. Yang, "Is a Good Representation Sufficient for Sample Efficient Reinforcement Learning?" arXiv preprint arXiv:1910.03016, 2019.

Dulac-Arnold, Gabriel, Nir Levine, Daniel J. Mankowitz, Jerry Li, Cosmin Paduraru, Sven Gowal, and Todd Hester, "Challenges of Real-World Reinforcement Learning: Definitions, Benchmarks and Analysis," *Machine Learning*, Vol. 110, No. 9, 2021.

"Duty of Care," *Oxford Reference* entry, Oxford University Press, undated.

Faul, Anita C., *A Concise Introduction to Machine Learning*, CRC Press, 2019.

Fedus, William, Jeff Dean, and Barret Zoph, "A Review of Sparse Expert Models in Deep Learning," arXiv preprint arXiv:2209.01667, 2022.

Fridman, Lex, "MIT 6.S091: Introduction to Deep Reinforcement Learning (Deep RL)," video, 2019. As of September 28, 2023:
https://www.youtube.com/watch?v=zR11FLZ-O9M&list=PLrAXtmErZgOeiKm4sgNOknGvNjby9efdf

"Game Theory in Tic Tac Toe," *Networks* blog, Cornell University, October 21, 2015. As of October 5, 2023:
https://blogs.cornell.edu/info2040/2015/10/21/game-theory-in-tic-tac-toe/

Garcia, Javier, and Fernando Fernández, "A Comprehensive Survey on Safe Reinforcement Learning," *Journal of Machine Learning Research*, Vol. 16, No. 1, 2015.

Gleave, Adam, Michael Dennis, Cody Wild, Neel Kant, Sergey Levine, and Stuart Russell, "Adversarial Policies," webpage, GitHub, undated. As of October 6, 2023:
https://adversarialpolicies.github.io/

Glickman, Mark E., and Albyn C. Jones, "Rating the Chess Rating System," Boston University, 1999.

Grace, Katja, John Salvatier, Allan Dafoe, Baobao Zhang, and Owain Evans, "When Will AI Exceed Human Performance? Evidence from AI Experts," *Journal of Artificial Intelligence Research*, Vol. 62, 2018.

Gray, Drew, "Introducing Voyage Deepdrive," *Voyage*, November 13, 2019.

Guo, James, Ed Walker, and Congcong Li, "Seeing Is Knowing: Advances in Search and Image Recognition Train Waymo's Self-Driving Technology for Any Encounter," *Waypoint* blog, Waymo, February 6, 2020. As of October 9, 2023: https://blog.waymo.com/2020/02/content-search.html

Hailu, G., and G. Sommer, "On Amount and Quality of Bias in Reinforcement Learning," *Proceedings of the 1999 IEEE International Conference on Systems, Man, and Cybernetics* (Cat. No. 99CH37028), Vol. 722, 1999.

Hammoudeh, Ahmad, "A Concise Introduction to Reinforcement Learning," Princess Suamaya University for Technology, 2018.

Harris, Mark, "Google Has Spent over $1.1 Billion on Self-Driving Tech," *IEEE Spectrum*, September 15, 2017.

Harris, Sean, "Cruise's Continuous Learning Machine Predicts the Unpredictable on San Francisco Roads," *Cruise*, September 10, 2020.

Hassler, Susan, "Marvin Minsky and the Pursuit of Machine Understanding: Making Machines—and People—Think [Spectral Lines]," *IEEE Spectrum*, Vol. 53, No. 3, 2016.

Hawkins, Andrew J., "Intel's Mobileye Begins Testing Autonomous Vehicles in New York City," *The Verge*, July 20, 2021a.

Hawkins, Andrew J., "Intel Is Taking Its Self-Driving Company Mobileye Public in 2022," *The Verge*, December 7, 2021b.

Henderson, Peter, Riashat Islam, Philip Bachman, Joelle Pineau, Doina Precup, and David Meger, "Deep Reinforcement Learning That Matters," paper presented at Thirty-Second Association for the Advancement of Artificial Intelligence Conference on Artificial Intelligence (AAAI-18), New Orleans, Louisiana, February 2–7, 2018.

Hochreiter, Sepp, "Toward a Broad AI," *Communications of the ACM*, Association for Computing Machinery, Vol. 65, No. 4, 2022.

Holt, Charles A., and Alvin E. Roth, "The Nash Equilibrium: A Perspective," *Proceedings of the National Academy of Sciences*, Vol. 101, No. 12, 2004.

Hsu, Feng-Hsiung, "IBM's Deep Blue Chess Grandmaster Chips," *IEEE Micro*, Vol. 19, No. 2, 1999.

Hussein, Ahmed, Mohamed Medhat Gaber, Eyad Elyan, and Chrisina Jayne, "Imitation Learning: A Survey of Learning Methods," *ACM Computing Surveys*, Vol. 50, No. 2, 2017.

Ilahi, I., M. Usama, J. Qadir, M. U. Janjua, A. Al-Fuqaha, D. T. Hoang, and D. Niyato, "Challenges and Countermeasures for Adversarial Attacks on Deep Reinforcement Learning," *IEEE Transactions on Artificial Intelligence*, Vol. 3, No. 2, 2022.

Ilyas, Andrew, Shibani Santurkar, Dimitris Tsipras, Logan Engstrom, Brandon Tran, and Aleksander Madry, "Adversarial Examples Are Not Bugs, They Are Features," *Advances in Neural Information Processing Systems*, Vol. 32, 2019.

Intel, "Intel Announces Intent to Take Mobileye Public," press release, December 6, 2021.

Ivanov, Andrei, Nikoli Dryden, Tal Ben-Nun, Shigang Li, and Torsten Hoefler, "Data Movement Is All You Need: A Case Study on Optimizing Transformers," *Proceedings of Machine Learning and Systems*, Vol. 3, 2021.

Jie, Zhou, Zeng Zhiying, and Li Li, "A Meta-Analysis of Watson for Oncology in Clinical Application," *Scientific Reports*, Vol. 11, No. 1, March 11, 2021.

Jing, Pengfei, Qiyi Tang, Yuefeng Du, Lei Xue, Xiapu Luo, Ting Wang, Sen Nie, and Shi Wu, "Too Good to Be Safe: Tricking Lane Detection in Autonomous Driving with Crafted Perturbations," *Proceedings of USENIX Security Symposium*, 2021.

JJRicks Studios, "Waymo Self Driving Taxi Goes Rogue: Blocks Traffic, Evades Capture | JJRicks Rides with Waymo #54," video, May 12, 2021.

Johanson, Michael, "Measuring the Size of Large No-Limit Poker Games," arXiv preprint arXiv:1302.7008, 2013.

Johnson, Bonnie, and William A. Treadway, "Artificial Intelligence—an Enabler of Naval Tactical Decision Superiority," *AI Magazine*, Vol. 40, No. 1, 2019.

Jouppi, Norman P., Cliff Young, Nishant Patil, David Patterson, Gaurav Agrawal, Raminder Bajwa, Sarah Bates, Suresh Bhatia, Nan Boden, and Al Borchers, "In-Datacenter Performance Analysis of a Tensor Processing Unit," *Proceedings of the 44th Annual International Symposium on Computer Architecture*, 2017.

Khachadoorian, Angelle, Air Force Culture and Language Center, Maxwell Air Force Base, "Speaking Air Forcefully: The Gonculator Knows Best," March 18, 2022.

Koch, Christof, "How the Computer Beat the Go Player," *Scientific American Mind*, July 1, 2016.

Kumar, Aviral, Joey Hong, Anikait Singh, and Sergey Levine, "When Should We Prefer Offline Reinforcement Learning over Behavioral Cloning?" arXiv preprint arXiv:2204.05618, 2022.

Kumar, Ram Shankar Siva, David O. Brien, Kendra Albert, Salomé Viljöen, and Jeffrey Snover, "Failure Modes in Machine Learning Systems," arXiv preprint arXiv:1911.11034, 2019.

Ladosz, Pawel, Lilian Weng, Minwoo Kim, and Hyondong Oh, "Exploration in Deep Reinforcement Learning: A Survey," *Information Fusion*, Vol. 85, September 2022.

Lantz, Frank, Aaron Isaksen, Alexander Jaffe, Andy Nealen, and Julian Togelius, *Depth in Strategic Games*, Association for the Advancement of Artificial Intelligence, 2017.

Le Mero, Luc, Dewei Yi, Mehrdad Dianati, and Alexandros Mouzakitis, "A Survey on Imitation Learning Techniques for End-to-End Autonomous Vehicles," *IEEE Transactions on Intelligent Transportation Systems*, Vol. 23, No. 9, September 2022.

Levine, Sergey, Aviral Kumar, George Tucker, and Justin Fu, "Offline Reinforcement Learning: Tutorial, Review, and Perspectives on Open Problems," arXiv preprint arXiv:2005.01643, 2020.

Li, Yuxi, "Reinforcement Learning in Practice: Opportunities and Challenges," arXiv preprint arXiv:2202.11296, 2022.

Lichess, homepage, undated. As of October 5, 2023:
https://lichess.org/

Lingel, Sherrill, Jeff Hagen, Eric Hastings, Mary Lee, Matthew Sargent, Matthew Walsh, Li Ang Zhang, and David Blancett, *Joint All-Domain Command and Control for Modern Warfare: An Analytic Framework for Identifying and Developing Artificial Intelligence Applications*, RAND Corporation, RR-A4408/1-AF, 2020. As of September 29, 2023:
https://www.rand.org/pubs/research_reports/RR4408z1.html

Liu, Y., C. Wu, X. Xi, Y. Li, G. Cao, W. Cao, and H. Wang, "Adversarial Discriminative Feature Separation for Generalization in Reinforcement Learning," *Proceedings of the 2022 International Joint Conference on Neural Networks (IJCNN)*, 2022.

Lu, Yunlong, and Wenxin Li, "Techniques and Paradigms in Modern Game AI Systems," *Algorithms*, Vol. 15, No. 8, 2022.

Luccioni, Alexandra Sasha, Sylvain Viguier, and Anne-Laure Ligozat, "Estimating the Carbon Footprint of BLOOM, a 176B Parameter Language Model," arXiv preprint arXiv:2211.02001, 2022.

Luo, Fan-Ming, Tian Xu, Hang Lai, Xiong-Hui Chen, Weinan Zhang, and Yang Yu, "A Survey on Model-Based Reinforcement Learning," eprint arXiv:2206.0932, June 2022.

Marchau, Vincent A. W. J., Warren E. Walker, Pieter J. T. M. Bloemen, and Steven W. Popper, *Decision Making Under Deep Uncertainty: From Theory to Practice*, Springer Nature, 2019.

Mawakana, Tekedra, "Partnering with UPS to Deliver on Our Mission," *Waypoint* blog, Waymo, January 29, 2020. As of October 6, 2023:
https://blog.waymo.com/2020/01/partnering-with-ups-to-deliver-on-our.html

Mayer, Lauren A., Jon Schmid, Sydney Litterer, and Marjory S. Blumenthal, *A Structured Elicitation Approach to Identify Technology-Based Challenges: With Application to Inform Force Planning for Technological Surprise*, RAND Corporation, RR-A701-1, 2021. As of October 3, 2023:
https://www.rand.org/pubs/research_reports/RRA701-1.html

McLeod, Saul, "Skinner-Operant Conditioning," Simply Psychology, 2007.

Microsoft, "Build AI Without Data Science," webpage, undated. As of October 9, 2023:
https://www.microsoft.com/en-us/ai/autonomous-systems-project-bonsai?activetab=pivot%3aprimaryr7

Mirhoseini, Azalia, Anna Goldie, Mustafa Yazgan, Joe Wenjie Jiang, Ebrahim Songhori, Shen Wang, Young-Joon Lee, Eric Johnson, Omkar Pathak, and Azade Nazi, "A Graph Placement Methodology for Fast Chip Design," *Nature*, Vol. 594, No. 7862, 2021.

Mitrović, Sandra, Davide Andreoletti, and Omran Ayoub, "ChatGPT or Human? Detect and Explain. Explaining Decisions of Machine Learning Model for Detecting Short ChatGPT-Generated Text," arXiv preprint arXiv:2301.13852, 2023.

Mobileye, "Japan: Yoshida Taxi Company Lowers Collisions Rates by 85% with Mobileye Technology," webpage, undated-a. As of October 3, 2023:
https://www.mobileye.com/uk/fleets/case-study/japan-yoshida-taxi-company-lowers-collisions-rates-by-85-with-mobileye-technology/

Mobileye, "Rethinking Technology for the Autonomous Future," webpage, undated-b. As of October 3, 2023:
https://www.mobileye.com/our-technology/

Monett, Dagmar, Colin W. P. Lewis, and Kristinn R. Thórisson, eds., "On Defining Artificial Intelligence," special issue, *Journal of Artificial General Intelligence*, Vol. 11, No. 2, March 2, 2020.

Moos, Janosch, Kay Hansel, Hany Abdulsamad, Svenja Stark, Debora Clever, and Jan Peters, "Robust Reinforcement Learning: A Review of Foundations and Recent Advances," *Machine Learning and Knowledge Extraction*, Vol. 4, No. 1, 2022.

Myerson, Roger B., "Nash Equilibrium and the History of Economic Theory," *Voprosy Economiki*, Vol. 6, 2010.

National Institute of Standards and Technology, "Artificial Intelligence Risk Management Framework (AI RMF 1.0)," 2023.

Nowé, Ann, Peter Vrancx, and Yann-Michaël De Hauwere, "Game Theory and Multi-Agent Reinforcement Learning," in M. Wiering and M. van Otterlo, eds., *Reinforcement Learning. Adaptation, Learning, and Optimization*, Vol. 12, Springer, 2012.

Nuro, "Find a Career That Delivers," webpage, undated. As of October 6, 2023: https://www.nuro.ai/careers

Oak Ridge National Laboratory, "Frontier: Direction of Discovery," webpage, U.S. Department of Energy, undated. As of October 5, 2023: https://www.olcf.ornl.gov/frontier/

Ontañón, Santiago, Gabriel Synnaeve, Alberto Uriarte, Florian Richoux, David Churchill, and Mike Preuss, "RTS AI Problems and Techniques," in Newton Lee, ed., *Encyclopedia of Computer Graphics and Games*, Springer International Publishing, 2015.

OpenAI, "Introducing ChatGPT," *ChatGPT* blog, November 30, 2022. As of February 24, 2023: https://openai.com/blog/chatgpt

Owen, Louis, "Bird's-Eye View of Reinforcement Learning Algorithms Taxonomy," *Towards Data Science*, October 30, 2020.

Ozdaglar, Asuman E., "Strategic Form Games and Nash Equilibrium," in J. Baillicul and T. Samad, eds., *Encyclopedia of Systems and Control*, Springer, 2013.

Padakandla, Sindhu, "A Survey of Reinforcement Learning Algorithms for Dynamically Varying Environments," *ACM Computing Surveys*, Vol. 54, No. 6, 2021.

Pal, C. V., and F. Leon, "Brief Survey of Model-Based Reinforcement Learning Techniques," *Proceedings of the 24th International Conference on System Theory, Control and Computing (ICSTCC)*, 2020.

Patterson, David, Joseph Gonzalez, Quoc Le, Chen Liang, Lluis-Miquel Munguia, Daniel Rothchild, David So, Maud Texier, and Jeff Dean, "Carbon Emissions and Large Neural Network Training," arXiv preprint arXiv:2104.10350, 2021.

Plaat, Aske, *Learning to Play: Reinforcement Learning and Games*, Springer Nature, 2020.

Polonski, Vyacheslav, "People Don't Trust AI—Here's How We Can Change That," *Scientific American*, Vol. 10, 2018.

Prudencio, Rafael Figueiredo, Marcos R. O. A. Maximo, and Esther Luna Colombini, "A Survey on Offline Reinforcement Learning: Taxonomy, Review, and Open Problems," arXiv preprint arXiv:2203.01387, 2022.

Przybylko, Marcin, *Stochastic Games and Their Complexities*, Nouvelle Calédonie, 2019.

Qin, Zhiwei, Xiaocheng Tang, Yan Jiao, Fan Zhang, Zhe Xu, Hongtu Zhu, and Jieping Ye, "Ride-Hailing Order Dispatching at Didi via Reinforcement Learning," *INFORMS Journal on Applied Analytics*, Vol. 50, No. 5, 2020.

Rawat, Waseem, and Zenghui Wang, "Deep Convolutional Neural Networks for Image Classification: A Comprehensive Review," *Neural Computation*, Vol. 29, No. 9, September 1, 2017.

Salles, Arleen, Kathinka Evers, and Michele Farisco, "Anthropomorphism in AI," *AJOB Neuroscience*, Vol. 11, No. 2, 2020.

Sanjaya, Ricky, Jun Wang, and Yaodong Yang, "Measuring the Non-Transitivity in Chess," *Algorithms*, Vol. 15, No. 5, 2022.

Shafahi, Ali, W. Ronny Huang, Christoph Studer, Soheil Feizi, and Tom Goldstein, "Are Adversarial Examples Inevitable?" paper presented at the Seventh International Conference on Learning Representations, New Orleans, Louisiana, May 7, 2019.

Shalev-Shwartz, Shai, Shaked Shammah, and Amnon Shashua, "Safe, Multi-Agent, Reinforcement Learning for Autonomous Driving," arXiv preprint arXiv:1610.03295, October 11, 2016.

Shalev-Shwartz, Shai, Shaked Shammah, and Amnon Shashua, "On a Formal Model of Safe and Scalable Self-Driving Cars," Mobileye, 2017.

Shankar, Sadasivan, and Albert Reuther, "Trends in Energy Estimates for Computing in AI/ Machine Learning Accelerators, Supercomputers, and Compute-Intensive Applications," *Proceedings of the 2022 IEEE High Performance Extreme Computing Conference (HPEC)*, 2022.

Shyam, Radhey, and Ria Singh, "A Taxonomy of Machine Learning Techniques," *Journal of Advancements in Robotics*, Vol. 8, December 28, 2021.

Silver, David, Aja Huang, Chris J. Maddison, Arthur Guez, Laurent Sifre, George van den Driessche, Julian Schrittwieser, Ioannis Antonoglou, Veda Panneershelvam, Marc Lanctot, Sander Dieleman, Dominik Grewe, John Nham, Nal Kalchbrenner, Ilya Sutskever, Timothy Lillicrap, Madeleine Leach, Koray Kavukcuoglu, Thore Graepel, and Demis Hassabis, "Mastering the Game of Go with Deep Neural Networks and Tree Search," *Nature*, Vol. 529, No. 7587, January 1, 2016.

Silver, David, Julian Schrittwieser, Karen Simonyan, Ioannis Antonoglou, Aja Huang, Arthur Guez, Thomas Hubert, Lucas Baker, Matthew Lai, Adrian Bolton, Yutian Chen, Timothy Lillicrap, Fan Hui, Laurent Sifre, George van den Driessche, Thore Graepel, and Demis Hassabis, "Mastering the Game of Go Without Human Knowledge," *Nature*, Vol. 550, No. 7676, October 1, 2017.

Solan, Eilon, and Nicolas Vieille, "Stochastic Games," *Proceedings of the National Academy of Sciences*, Vol. 112, No. 45, 2015.

Somashekhar, S. P., Martín-J. Sepúlveda, Andrew D. Norden, Amit Rauthan, Kumar Arun, Poonam Patil, Ramya Y. Ethadka, and Rohit C. Kumar, "Early Experience with IBM Watson for Oncology (WFO) Cognitive Computing System for Lung and Colorectal Cancer Treatment," *Journal of Clinical Oncology*, Vol. 35, No. 15, Supp., 2017.

Song, Xingyou, Yiding Jiang, Stephen Tu, Yilun Du, and Behnam Neyshabur, "Observational Overfitting in Reinforcement Learning," arXiv preprint arXiv:1912.02975, 2019.

Srinivasan, Ramya, and Ajay Chander, "Biases in AI Systems," *Communications of the ACM*, Vol. 64, No. 8, 2021.

Stephenson, Matthew, Diego Perez-Liebana, Mark Nelson, Ahmed Khalifa, and Alexander Zook, "Game Complexity vs Strategic Depth," matthewstephenson.info, 2019.

Strickland, Eliza, "IBM Watson, Heal Thyself: How IBM Overpromised and Underdelivered on AI Health Care," *IEEE Spectrum*, Vol. 56, No. 4, 2019.

Szegedy, Christian, Wojciech Zaremba, Ilya Sutskever, Joan Bruna, Dumitru Erhan, Ian J. Goodfellow, and Rob Fergus, "Intriguing Properties of Neural Networks," arXiv preprint arXiv:1312.6199, 2014.

Thompson, N. C., K. Greenewald, K. Lee, and G. F. Manso, "Deep Learning's Diminishing Returns: The Cost of Improvement Is Becoming Unsustainable," *IEEE Spectrum*, Vol. 58, No. 10, 2021.

Threewitt, Cherise, "10 Vehicles That Are Almost Self-Driving in 2023," *U.S. News and World Report*, April 20, 2023.

Udugama, B., "Review of Deep Reinforcement Learning for Autonomous Driving," arXiv preprint arXiv:2302.06370, 2023.

Ummels, Michael, and Dominik Wojtczak, "The Complexity of Nash Equilibria in Simple Stochastic Multiplayer Games," paper presented at Automata, Languages and Programming: 36th International Colloquium, ICALP 2009, Rhodes, Greece, July 5–12, 2009.

U.S. Energy Information Administration, *Annual Electric Power Industry Report*, EIA-861, 2021.

Victor, Trent, Kristofer Kusano, Tilia Gode, Ruoshu Chen, and Matthew Schwall, *Safety Performance of the Waymo Rider-Only Automated Driving System at One Million Miles*, Waymo, 2023.

"Voyage Launches Open-Source Self-Driving Simulation Platform," *Robotics Business Review*, November 14, 2019.

Walz, Eric, "Waymo Is Deploying Its Self-Driving Vehicles in New York City," *FutureCar*, December 10, 2021.

Wang, Ruosong, Yifan Wu, Ruslan Salakhutdinov, and Sham Kakade, "Instabilities of Offline RL with Pre-Trained Neural Representation," *Proceedings of the International Conference on Machine Learning*, 2021.

Warren, Tom, "Intel Acquiring Mobileye's Self-Driving Car Technology in $15 Billion Deal," *The Verge*, March 13, 2017.

Waymo, homepage, undated. As of October 9, 2023:
https://waymo.com

Waymo, "Same Driver, Different Vehicle: Bringing Waymo Self-Driving Technology to Trucks," *Waypoint* blog, March 9, 2018. As of October 6, 2023:
https://blog.waymo.com/2019/08/same-driver-different-vehicle-bringing.html

Waymo, "The Waymo Driver's Training Regimen: How Structured Testing Prepares Our Self-Driving Technology for the Real World," *Waypoint* blog, September 10, 2020. As of October 3, 2023:
https://blog.waymo.com/2020/09/the-waymo-drivers-training-regime.html

Waymo, "Waymo Via Is Working with J. B. Hunt to Carry Freight Across Texas," *Waypoint* blog, June 10, 2021a. As of October 6, 2023:
https://blog.waymo.com/2021/06/waymo-via-is-working-with-jb-hunt-to.html

Waymo, "Scale AI's TransformX Presentation with Waymo Head of Research Drago Anguelov," video, October 20, 2021b. As of October 3, 2023:
https://www.youtube.com/watch?v=oJ96bgmSaW0

Westenberger, Jens, Kajetan Schuler, and Dennis Schlegel, "Failure of AI Projects: Understanding the Critical Factors," *Procedia Computer Science*, Vol. 196, 2022.

Williams, Robert, and Roman Yampolskiy, "Understanding and Avoiding AI Failures: A Practical Guide," *Philosophies*, Vol. 6, No. 3, 2021.

Winters, Ryan, Andrew Winters, and Ronald G. Amedee, "Statistics: A Brief Overview," *Ochsner Journal*, Vol. 10, No. 3, 2010.

Yaghoobzadehtari, Sina, Colin Owusu Adomako, and Siavash Paidar, "Elaborate Operational Requirements to Address Reward Hacking in Reinforcement Learning Agents," thesis, Chalmers University of Technology and University of Gothenberg, 2019.

Yang, Rui, Chenjia Bai, Xiaoteng Ma, Zhaoran Wang, Chongjie Zhang, and Lei Han, "RORL: Robust Offline Reinforcement Learning via Conservative Smoothing," arXiv preprint arXiv:2206.02829, 2022.

Yin, Qiyue, Jun Yang, Wancheng Ni, Bin Liang, and Kaiqi Huang, "AI in Games: Techniques, Challenges and Opportunities," arXiv preprint arXiv:2111.07631, 2021.

Yvkoff, Liane, "With Acquisition of Latent Logic, Waymo Adds Imitation Learning to Self-Driving Training," *Forbes*, December 12, 2019.

Zhou, K., Z. Liu, Y. Qiao, T. Xiang, and C. C. Loy, "Domain Generalization: A Survey," *IEEE Transactions on Pattern Analysis and Machine Intelligence*, Vol. 45, No. 4, 2023.

Zhou, Zixuan, Shushu Yi, and Jie Zhang, "Survey on Storage-Accelerator Data Movement," *CCF Transactions on High Performance Computing*, Vol. 4, 2022.

Zhu, Z., and H. Zhao, "A Survey of Deep RL and IL for Autonomous Driving Policy Learning," *IEEE Transactions on Intelligent Transportation Systems*, Vol. 23, No. 9, 2022.